This book tells you everything you need to know to make an 8mm or 16mm movie, but it doesn't tell you "how-to", because Rodger Larson doesn't believe in telling young filmmakers "how-to." At the very base of his teaching has been his conviction that the creative directions of young filmmakers should determine the way they will go.

The opening sections describe some of the films teenagers are making today. Other sections deal with such matters as the nature of visual language, and the actual shooting of the picture beginning with formulation of an idea and script, including the responsibilities of the filmmaker as his own director and cameraman. All the necessary information about equipment is here, too, and full coverage of the editing process and ways to create a soundtrack.

But most importantly, the authors have translated into words the basic essentials of the filmmaking experience, helping young filmmakers understand how to use the technical means at their command to realize expressive ends. As Rodger Larson states in his Foreword: "Making movies gives you the chance to find out what you want to say and to say it in your own way."

YOUNG FILMMAKERS

YOUNG FILMMAKERS

By Rodger Larson with Ellen Meade

Original photographs by Marcelo Montealegre

E. P. DUTTON & CO., INC., NEW YORK

Published simultaneously in Canada by
Clarke, Irwin & Company Limited, Toronto and Vancouver

Library of Congress Catalog Card Number: 70-81724

Marcelo Montealegre's photographs appear on
frontispiece and pages 65, 78, 81, 84, 88, 97, 99, 102, 111,
114, 117, 118, 120, 122, 124, 126, 127, 134, 136, 141,
143, 145, 147, 149, 152, 155, 159, 161, 162, 168, 173

Appreciations

We are grateful to Bruce Spiegel, Director of Henry Street Movie Club, New York City, for his careful reading of the entire manuscript from a film teacher's point-of-view.

Peter Bradley, Film Program Director, New York State Council on the Arts, contributed intelligent suggestions throughout the book. Lynne Hofer and Jaime Barrios of the Young Filmaker's Foundation contributed ideas especially to the section dealing with visual language.

Film editor, Samuel Moore, provided us with the very useful index.

Doris Montealegre worked with painstaking attention in the darkroom assisting her husband in printing stills.

Contents

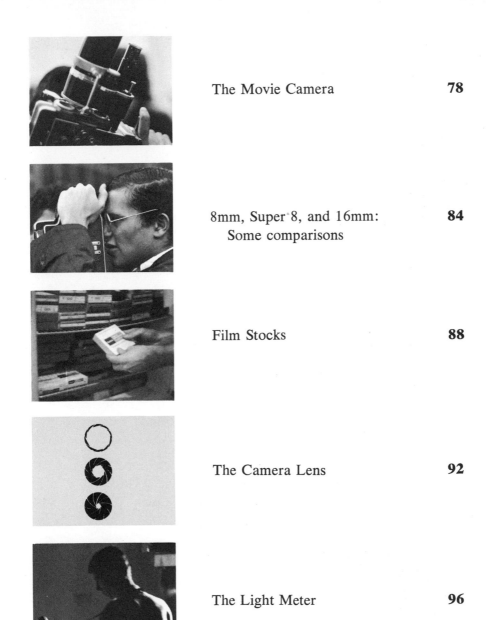

MAKING MOVIES PUTS YOU AT THE CENTER OF A GREAT DEAL OF FUN and action. In recent years I have watched many different kinds of people take delight in film equipment and what it can do; they are exhilarated by the prospect of transferring an idea from their imaginations to a screen.

In 1963 I was working with a group of teen-agers in the Summer Theatre Arts Program at the Mosholu-Montefiore Community Center in the Bronx, New York. I proposed that we try some filmmaking on the side, and a few students pounced on the idea and ran away with it. Films emerged as the most vital part of our summer program. What happened to me as a result was that a year later I abandoned my job as an art teacher and was out of work for six months; I went from place to place trying to convince various organizations that filmmaking meant more to many teen-agers than any of the creative arts then being offered them. Finally I found a temporary base of operations at the 92nd Street YM-YWHA in New York City. A lot of the films I am going to tell you about were made by my students at the 92nd Street YM-YWHA and at the Mosholu-Montefiore Community Center.

By 1966 I had decided that I wanted to teach teen-agers in a permanent film workshop. FILM CLUB evolved from this need. It started out in the kitchen pantry of the University Settlement on New York's Lower East Side. Today it is a thriving independent unit supported by the Young Filmaker's Foundation. Almost forty films have been produced by the members.

There are several ways to go about making a movie. At FILM CLUB we made *The Revenge—Teenagers Western Style* as a collaborative effort by students and adults. Members, their friends, relatives, and teachers all pitched in. The jobs ranged from script writing

◀ *The Revenge—Teenagers Western Style*

through camera operation and acting to composing an original score and editing. The film showed the marks of many different people, and they in turn were whistling its theme song for months. I have also seen films made entirely by teen-agers as class projects; in fact, my art class made a painted film. Except for this and *The Revenge,* in which adults participated, my students have chosen to work individually or occasionally in pairs. The filmmaker or co-filmmakers are fully responsible for the finished movie, but they may call upon their friends and other students to act in their productions and to assist them technically. Although students working in pairs often have strong differences of opinion, the give-and-take can produce lively results. Teen-agers are usually wary of sharing their ideas with a co-author, and given the opportunity, would rather dominate their own films. Most of them prefer to work alone: they formulate an idea, script it, direct the actors, shoot and edit the footage, prepare screen credits and a sound track, and eventually present the finished film to an audience.

Two movie directors give me the same sense of joy that I get from my students. Both men are prime contributors to the growth of filmmaking. Andy Warhol and the late D. W. Griffith share a startling originality. They approach film as if no one had ever made a movie before. I think young people have this same independence, and it becomes them.

Young Filmmakers grew out of my experience with my students. In writing it I thought out loud and at random while my co-author, writer Ellen Meade, listened. But not for long. Her spells of quietly making notes were frequently interrupted as her eyes narrowed to slits and she zoomed in with questions like "What *are* you talking about?" I think she has a lot of wisdom about people, but she really did not know very much about filmmaking. When we agreed that what we were committing to paper made sense to both of us, we felt hopeful that our readers would also understand the fundamentals of filmmaking.

Making movies gives you the chance to be your own boss, to find out what you want to say and to say it in your own way. Whether or not you are planning to make a film, think of yourself as a film-maker as you read this book.

—Rodger Larson

New York City
March, 1969

THE MOVIE ANY TEEN-AGER CHOOSES TO MAKE DEPENDS, I THINK, on a lot of things—where he is in our society, where he lives, who his family is, what school he goes to; they shape his film as they shape the person he is. Fitting either film or filmmaker with a neat and exact label is impossible, yet just as people can be termed, in a very general way, extroverted or introverted, optimistic or pessimistic, artistic, intellectual, athletic, witty, or lazy, films can be described in terms of their dominant characteristics. I will give you examples of the kinds of movies I have known teen-agers to make, which should give you an idea of the scope of expression possible. The first group comes under the heading of *direct photography*.

Bubby is a *documentary*. It is a portrait of Bubby, the grandmother of an eighteen-year-old high-school senior named Murray. As a little boy, Murray lived with Bubby, and he has great love and respect for her; he looks quite a bit like her. In this film his special interest is in how Bubby, in her eighties, holds on to life. To get the footage, he stayed in her home and used available light. He filmed her just as she was, doing the things she usually did: eating, washing dishes, napping, watching television, walking slowly from room to room, looking at herself in a mirror, looking out the window. These shots were intercut with shots of the setting sun and of photographs on her wall; the photographs covered sixty years of her life and showed her, her husband (who had died), and her children.

Two thirds of the way through the film, following a shot of the photo of her husband as a young man, is a shot of a young anonymous girl standing by a river. Shots of the rushing river as it splashes over rocks and logs are then intercut with those of the grandmother moving about her house. As she walks toward her sink, there are cuts

17

◀ *Bubby*

to a clump of grass being carried by the river to the edge of a waterfall. When the grass flows over the edge, she reaches out her hand toward the tap and shuts it off, stopping its dripping. This is the end of the movie.

The limitations of a documentary lie in the necessity to take it as it comes. Murray could not ask his grandmother to do anything she did not ordinarily do. The satisfaction in making a documentary is in recording a personality or subject or event without intruding upon it. The filmmaker must rely largely on his editing to express his point of view. Murray did this by intercutting the scenes of the river, which symbolizes the life force: when we see the clump of grass slip over the waterfall, we want to save it from being dashed to pieces at the bottom by holding back the rushing river. In the following shot of the old woman shutting off the dripping faucet we feel her need to hold back life's slipping away.

Murray's control of his subject was instinctive rather than intellectual. He included only one extreme close-up of his grandmother and kept his camera at a respectful distance the rest of the time. In the close-up, Bubby is eating, and her determination and concentration underline the intensity of her wish to survive; if the camera had been eight or ten feet away, the impact would not have been the same. Murray sensed this without analyzing it.

Fran's temperament is different from Murray's. Instead of focusing on someone else, she focused on herself and made an *autobiographical film*. Instead of working intuitively, she figured out ahead of time exactly what she would do and why. Fran was sixteen when she joined our film workshop, and she began by stating emphatically that she had had an unhappy experience the previous summer in a theatre-arts camp and wanted to tell about it. She had gone to theatre camp because she was interested in acting, but she had had to take

18

Diana ▶

a dance class. She said that she had felt like an "awful klutz" and that it had been one of the most painful times of her life.

Her film is called *Diana* after the Roman goddess of the hunt, whom Fran saw as a symbol of physical grace and beauty. The opening shot is of a very pretty girl (Diana) walking up to a large institutional building accompanied by the sound of a drum beating a monotonous, insistent rhythm. She walks alone down a long corridor in time to the drumbeat, as if to her own execution, and enters an empty white room, which has a ballet bar on the wall. Her face is full of dread. There is a close-up of a female hand beating the drum. The sound crescendos. Two girls are seen briefly, doing dance exercises at the bar with grace and pleasure. Back to the drum: the hand stops beating it and points an accusing finger at Diana, who swallows hard and begins a dance exercise; she is clumsy and nearly falls on her face.

The room darkens and she is in a spotlight. The drumbeat is replaced by melodious piano music. Diana dances beautifully for a few moments. The harsh white light and the drumbeat return, and she is back in dance class exercising awkwardly. Again she escapes into the ballerina fantasy and again is pulled back to the unhappy reality of dance class. Almost in tears she flees from the room. Next she is seen walking dejectedly outside the building. On the street there is a little girl who waves, rushes up to her, and hugs her. Hand in hand they run down the street in slow motion to the melodious strains of the piano.

I have never known exactly what that ending means. It is a good example of how the filmmaker can communicate visually to the viewer and the viewer can feel that he gets the message yet not be able to say what it is. Is that little girl real or imagined? Was she waiting for Diana or are they strangers? Is Fran saying that Diana will be fulfilled as a mother and not as a dancer? Or that she wishes she were a little girl again? Is there another explanation? I cannot tell you, but for me the ending feels coherent with the rest of the film.

Diana demonstrates how the facts of a personal experience can be translated into a film that is not a literal reenactment but rather a highly subjective rendition. This requires sensitive use of camera techniques. In the shot where Diana is walking down the corridor, a telephoto lens distorted the perspective, so that she seems to be taking innumerable steps without getting anywhere: the corridor appears shorter than it really was, but the actress takes as many steps to traverse it as she had needed to traverse the actual long corridor. Thus Fran conveyed her heroine's leadenness and reluctance to go to class. Diana and the little girl running together at the end in slow motion seem to float with almost supernatural grace. Fran knew what she was doing when she decided on these techniques. She intended to communicate her feelings about dance class rather than to report on what that dance class was like.

Of course, an autobiographical film can be an earnest attempt by the filmmaker to re-create down to the smallest detail a true personal experience.

Memory of John Earl is such a film. John was born and raised in South Carolina. When he was eighteen, he came to Middletown, Connecticut, with an aunt because they had had enough of being black in the deep South. John has little formal education, but he is a poet and has always been interested in the arts. He joined an Upward Bound project at Wesleyan University because it offered a chance to study theatre and filmmaking. John does not care about his inability to add and subtract ("I can tell when I'm being cheated—I don't need to count my change"), but he is acquiring the verbal skills needed for writing poetry and film scripts.

When I first saw his film at a Filmmakers' Happening in New York

City, it impressed me, so I talked to him about it afterward. He said that the story had actually happened to him and that he had often wished he could make a movie about it. In response to the request for plot ideas from his film teacher in Upward Bound, John told about his experience; the class was hypnotized. They decided to do it as a film for their summer project.

Memory of John Earl is set in South Carolina, and in it John plays his fourteen-year-old self. With three friends he goes to a small country store to get a snack. The white storekeeper's white wife is behind the counter and is afraid of them. She calls her husband, who cuts a fifteen-cent slice of meat for John and throws it on the counter. John objects to his manner and the man begins insulting the boys. John is determined to keep his dignity as a person and stands up to the man while the other boys slink away. The man grows more excited and John finally says he won't let anyone talk to him that way when he's done nothing wrong. The storekeeper comes around the counter, grabs John by the collar, and throws him out the door and down the front steps, calling to his wife to bring the shotgun. John's friends are waiting in a panel truck which they have driven into town from the fields where they work. John joins them just as the wife appears with a shotgun.

The film manages to be funny when the man discovers that the gun he is aiming at John has no shells. He curses at the gun and yells at his wife to bring ammunition. The boys do not wait for her to obey—they drive off. The storekeeper will not give up easily. He mobilizes his two sons and they give chase in a car. John's friends, afraid for their safety, urge him to leave them. He jumps from the truck and runs to hide. His pursuers follow. Exhausted, John falls to the ground in fear, his face and body bruised and bleeding. The three pursuers surround him as he cowers beneath the loaded gun. The storekeeper says, "We're going to get you later." They leave him

◀ *Memory of John Earl*

and he staggers to the road, where a white man is standing, having been a silent witness. He did nothing to help, and one senses that he dreaded getting involved. John looks as if he is going to cry. The man says, "We'd better get you to the doctor." End of film.

When a young filmmaker is plagued by the memory of a strong experience that he wants to get out of his system, he may feel better after turning the experience into a movie. John wants to do two sequels telling the rest of this true story. The second film would show the cruel and neglectful treatment John received from the doctor. The third would show the helplessness of the sympathetic lawyer whom he consulted and who tried to help him but who could not get a response from the Justice Department in Washington when he reported this chain of events.

The most obvious problem in filming the story was re-creating a small South Carolina town in New England. John knew his hometown so well that he was able to find a location similar to it in Middletown. The trick lies in selecting carefully when you shoot—a scene that looked appropriate on the screen would have been spoiled had a building just outside the frame been included.

This is the first film I have mentioned that needed even a few lines of dialogue. It was shot without sound in one day, from 8 A.M. to sundown; that could never have been done with synchronous sound because recording on location slows you down. Although this was a group project, John was very much involved in all phases of the production. He worked on the script, directed some scenes, acted in it, and took a big interest in the editing and dubbing. After two weeks of editing, the students were ready to add sound. John got native Southerners living in Middletown to provide the needed voices, since the actors did not have Southern accents. The townspeople were shown the film and matched their lines to the actors' lip movements. This reading was recorded on tape and transferred to an optical track. The voices have a strange distance from the film and sound slightly unreal, which adds to the impression that one is sharing a memory. There are also sound effects on the tape, and a little flute melody which was played by the actor who had impersonated the storekeeper. The movie is as accurate a re-creation of what happened to John as he and his friends could put on film.

An even more literally autobiographical film is *Looking Back* by Benjamin, who excerpted scenes from his father's home movies. We see Benjamin from infancy through childhood and finally as the seventeen-year-old he now is—all in six minutes. Besides doing the complex editing job, Benjamin photographed his bedroom and had his parents take a few current shots.

The next film is *narrative,* made by a seventeen-year-old high-school junior named Jesus, who came into FILM CLUB to work after school and on Saturdays. The first film he made was *An Unpleasant Evening.* When Jesus was ready to begin shooting, a very explicit story came quickly to mind:

A group of teen-agers arrives at their community center. The camera follows Chicky, who gets there after the others and wanders through the building looking for his friends. He runs into Rosalene, an unhappy girl who stands apart from the socializing. She gives him money—we don't know why—and while he goes back outside, she retreats to the girls' room. We then watch Chicky entering a liquor store and realize that Rosalene asked him to buy her wine and smuggle it into the building. When he hands her the bottle, she sheepishly accepts it and returns to the girls' room where she downs the contents in one long gulp.

She staggers into the hallway and is discovered there by her boy-friend, Ivan. He is furious that she is drunk, yells at her, pulls her hair

fiercely, and rejects her. Humiliated and hurt, Rosalene leaves the building. Ivan wants revenge. He finds out who got her the wine and with his friend, Chino, corners Chicky in the boys' room where they beat him up.

The entire movie takes only eight minutes. Teen-age films are rarely longer than ten minutes. These short films are to feature films what short stories are to novels. In the short narrative movie the tale is often told without the solid structure of beginning, middle, and end, which longer movies may depend on. The viewer comes into the life of a character, stays with him for an experience, and leaves him a while later.

A narrative film is first of all concerned with telling a story. *An Unpleasant Evening* was shown on an educational television program. Jesus and I also appeared, to discuss filmmaking. The interviewer for the show asked what the scene in which the girl drinks the wine "means." Jesus was prepared for just about any question, but that threw him. He thought the interviewer was either stupid or had not been paying attention to the film. He replied, "It means she drank the wine and she got drunk. I see that all the time." The interviewer hurried on to the next question.

Naturally Jesus' movie does "mean" more than the plot. Let's take the scene our television host chose, as an example. The first shot shows Rosalene drinking; woozy music on sound track; sharp cut to youngsters in lounge of community center, dancing and having fun; cut back to Rosalene alone with bottle. Translated into words, this segment says that instead of having teen-age friends, this lonely girl uses the bottle as a friend. This is clearly expressed in just three shots, which take ten seconds on screen. But Jesus could not talk about it in those terms to the interviewer because his language is visual.

There is a special challenge in the narrative film. You are telling a literal story which takes place in a specific amount of time, and if

◀ *An Unpleasant Evening*

it is going to be believed, there has to be continuity of detail. Jesus learned this the hard way, through experience. It was the wine bottle that gave him trouble. The day he was preparing to shoot Chicky giving the bottle to Rosalene he had assembled the actors and cameraman. The lights were set up. But he had forgotten that bottle. While everyone waited and fumed, he had to run outside and look for a wine bottle, fill it with water, and get food coloring to make the water look like wine. As a result of this forty-five-minute delay, the scene was not completed that day.

A few days later when shooting resumed he had lost the bottle. He got a different one. Still later, when he was editing, he realized that the second bottle had an obviously different label from the first one. He had to go back again and reshoot the first scenes using the second bottle, which he had carefully saved—just in case. Jesus has made other films, and he always likes a strong story to hang his intentions on; he pays close attention to details to make his stories seem real.

Movies and dreams have much in common. In both we move effortlessly through time and space. A *fantasy* film can take full advantage of this relationship and free the imagination from the limitations of reality. Jesus dealt with a continuous piece of time and believable events. Fran showed Diana's fantasy of being a graceful ballerina as a daydream in a realistic movie; she changed the lighting from bright to dark and the sound track from drumbeat to piano strains in order to emphasize that the scene was taking place separately, in Diana's imagination. Murray intercut shots of the rushing river to symbolize Bubby's intense love of life. Miguel, in the next film I want to describe, intended that we participate in the magical aspects of this fantasy.

Those Powerful Pills was Miguel's third film. His first two were

28

Those Powerful Pills ▶

Do You Love Me?, a melodrama, and *Male and Female,* a daydream. Miguel joined FILM CLUB when he was eighteen. He is the kind of person who likes the easy life and doing things his own way. His chief enjoyments are composing songs on his guitar, playing baseball, dating girls, and making movies, and he views them all as similar entertainments. His favorite ambition is to be leader of a rock group. While making films he works just hard enough to get the effects he needs and not one bit more. His attitude is that sweating is for peasants. As a result, his movies have a delightful playfulness about them.

Those Powerful Pills is about a young man who has the ability to become invisible when he chooses. He is X-rayed in a mobile X-ray van and his body chemistry mysteriously changes, so that afterward an ordinary aspirin makes him invisible. He discovers that he can do mischievous things when he can't be seen. He notices two tough guys walking down the street and is slightly afraid of them; he takes a pill and plays a joke on them by punching and pushing one of them who thinks his friend is hitting him and hits back; a fight is provoked.

As his visible self the boy is kicked off the basketball court by boys who think he is not a good player. He retaliates by becoming invisible and rejoining the game. He knocks about the team captain who had bullied him earlier, and the captain goes berserk. The team abandons the court. The boy is triumphant. The next shot is of the empty basketball court, and we don't know if the boy is there. Suddenly, with comic glee, his head pops out from behind a tree. Two pretty girls pass by, and in his enthusiasm he swallows all the pills left in the bottle, hoping to become superinvisible. He disappears, and we see only an open belt draped over the railing on which he had been sitting. A young man comes along holding up his too-large pants, looks around to see if anyone is watching, grabs the belt, and puts it on. His hands now free, he waves them happily as he skips

30

off. The original boy is doomed to remain forever a belt on another boy's pants.

Miguel did not need particularly complicated effects to create this fantasy. The boy was made to disappear through the use of a tripod to hold the camera absolutely steady while the film was stopped and the actor left the scene. Then the film rolled again, capturing exactly the same scene as a minute before but without the boy. On the screen he seems to vanish magically. Drawing the viewer into your film helps him to believe in the unbelievable. Miguel accomplished this partly by including a few shots taken as if through the hero's eyes. When the boy invisibly approaches the basketball court and when he spots the two girls, we see what he would see. This is called subjective camera.

Filmmakers should be flexible. Miguel originally planned to have the young man turn into a dog instead of a belt, but the day he shot that scene no dog was handy. Not being one to overexert himself, Miguel decided to use a belt. I think the final effect is stronger and more interesting than it would have been with a dog.

When Bill, a sixteen-year-old filmmaker, came to me with the script for his second film, I told him he had a rather morbid view of life and asked if he could not make a more wholesome film. He answered, "What if Dostoyevsky's writing teacher had told him that? Where would he be today?" So, sticking to the principle that you can make any film you want, I said okay. The movie was so gruesome that he could not get anyone to act in it, so he decided to do a movie version of Edgar Allan Poe's *The Tell-Tale Heart* instead. Armed with the authority of a minor classic, he gathered together his actors to make a *surrealistic* movie.

The opening shot is of two men sitting across from each other at a kitchen table eating lunch. The younger one hides behind his news-

32

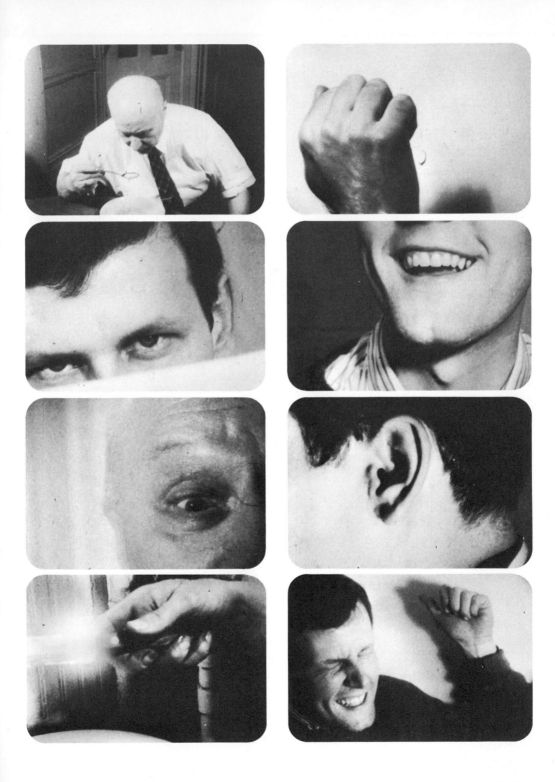

paper and from time to time peers out in agitation at the old man, who seems oblivious to everything except his chicken noodle soup. When the old man has left the room, the younger one looks into his own bowl and sees the old man's eye staring up at him from among the noodles; he grabs a knife and slashes at the soup. Next we see the old man sleeping in a darkened room. The young man sneaks up to him with a flashlight and shines it on his face: the sleeping man's right eye remains open. The young man becomes even more agitated and finally smothers the eye—and the man—with a pillow. The screen goes black.

There follows a series of extreme close-ups showing the dismemberment of the old man's body by the young man, ending with a puddle of blood being washed down the bathtub drain. We next see the murderer nailing floorboards in place; we imagine that the body is buried beneath them. Inexplicably a detective appears at the door. On the sound track a heartbeat is heard growing louder. There is a series of fast cuts jumping back and forth in time to the heartbeat between the floorboards and the murderer's ear, glazed eyes, and rapidly talking mouth. His mounting hysteria contrasts with the detective's bewilderment. The heartbeats continue in synchronization with the fast cuts until the murderer collapses and confesses.

Bill had photographed the detective taking the murderer away, but in the finished version he thought it more dramatic to end on the young man's complete breakdown. Bill assumed the audience would know the story already and did not feel obliged to explain the plot or where the detective came from. He was concerned with the passion of the murder and the murderer's overwhelming guilt. Probably the biggest influence on Bill in making this movie was Alfred Hitchcock's *Psycho*.

Surrealism attempts to convey the irrational fragmentation of the subconscious. The eye in the soup is a clear example of this. So are

34

the swift cuts and loud heartbeat, which portray the murderer's hysteria. At the beginning Bill wanted to use a glass eyeball in the soup, but he decided a lifelike eye which could blink would be more effective. He used a double exposure. The first shot was of the soup bowl. Then the film was wound back in the camera, and the second shot was of the old man's eye looking through an eye-shaped hole in black cardboard (only the eye registered on the film—the cardboard disappeared). The fast cuts were achieved in editing.

At fourteen Andy was playful and had a somewhat vitriolic sense of humor. He liked to poke fun at people, especially adults (me), but beneath his teasing was a basic affection. He was the first young filmmaker I met. He and his friend Randy had been making movies in 8mm since they were twelve. In the summer of 1963 when I began to work with teen-age filmmakers, Andy and Randy were the first to join my projected group. They were excited about meeting people who would share their enthusiasms. Andy presented me with a script, titled *That Rotten Teabag,* that I did not understand. It seemed disjointed and without point. He had listed shots clearly, but they had no apparent relation to one another. What did a man distributing handbills that told passersby to write their Congressmen have to do with a lady rushing home clutching a handbill, stopping to salute the American flag, then opening her pocketbook to find it stuffed with old tea bags? I thought I'd better show Andy how to use a 16mm camera and leave him alone. The three-minute film that emerged has been one of the most successful *social satires* I have ever seen. What Andy was saying was that hate is irrational. This accounts for the irrational construction of the script.

The film opens with an extreme close-up of a teakettle. We follow a young man who is preparing himself a cup of tea. As he sips the tea, the tea bag slips into the center of his saucer. He doesn't notice

35

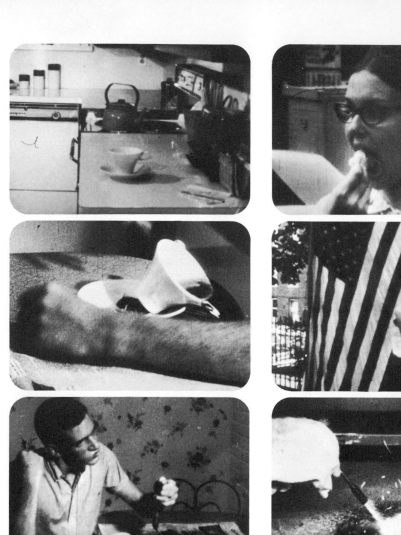

and sets his cup down on top of the tea bag. Naturally the cup tips, and it spills hot liquid down his leg. Furious, he shakes his fist at the soggy little thing. Next there is a cut to a young lady standing on a sidewalk drinking tea from a paper container. She walks to a litter basket and is about to drop the tea bag in when she sees a severely worded notice attached to it stating that it will not accept messy tea bags. The poor girl is in utter despair and has to eat the tea bag to get rid of it. Suddenly there seems to be a worldwide crusade to eliminate tea bags. This is indicated by a variety of fast cuts in which tea bags are torn apart, stomped on, hammered, squeezed, cut, and burned, ending with a shot of a tombstone.

Most audiences are reduced to a kind of helpless laughter by Andy's film, partly because it seems so improbable. The most effective humor often deals with serious, sad, or even terrifying subjects. Beneath the surface of this wacky, comic spoof of protest and patriotism there is a somber message. After watching the movie quite a few times, I began to sense that Andy's film was about prejudice. I asked him if this was so. He said that no such thought had been in his mind. I don't overinterpret films, but this particular one just kept nagging at me. A few years later *That Rotten Teabag* was seen by black audiences in Harlem during a Moviebus program that showed teen-age movies on city streets. While black teen-agers enjoyed all the other films, this one was universally disliked. There was no laughter; instead there were boos and hisses. Andy was on the Moviebus and was startled that a film that had always provoked hilarity suddenly provoked anger. It seemed obvious to all of us that the Harlem teen-agers identified with the tea bags. Andy told himself something with visual language that he had been unable to tell himself with words.

The snappy, zesty pace of Andy's film is important to its success. It was photographed at sixteen frames per second (FPS), and because he was too easily satisfied, it was sluggish. When he put it on

◀ *That Rotten Teabag*

a sound speed projector to add a sound track, the action had to be speeded up fifty percent. If he had filmed at the 24FPS necessary with a sound track, he would have had to cut short his shots to achieve the liveliness that the film now has. Not only was the tempo positively affected by running the film more quickly through the projector than it had been run through the camera, but the figures move with a frenzy that adds a lot of humor.

The End has perplexed me throughout the writing of this section. At first I thought it was narrative, then fantasy, then social satire. But it refused to be stuck with any label. Since it is such an original movie, I am anxious to mention it and have stopped worrying about a category. Call it what you will. I call it great.

The filmmaker is Alfonso, and at nineteen he had made three films. He writes his scripts in a fine hand, neat, tight, and sharp. The movies come out the same way. They are beautifully constructed and very telling. *The End,* his third film, candidly expresses how he feels about social forces that surround and sometimes press upon him. The film begins with his good friend, Benny, and a poster showing President Johnson astride a motorcycle (it is one of those posters made by putting together bits of photographs to make a fake picture). Alfonso had cut a slit over the President's pocket, and the first shot shows Benny lifting a joint of marijuana out of that pocket. Benny lights the joint and falls into a marijuana reverie in which he becomes a song-and-dance man with two lovely girl partners. Then without warning he is thrust behind the steering wheel of a broken-down auto, and he tries to kid himself that he's driving a high-powered sports car. As his reverie progresses, Benny's wish for a happy world is captured in a newspaper headline that announces the legalization of marijuana. He kicks up his heels and jumps for joy. Two men appear, one a grubby angel who thrusts the Bible into his hand, the other an attrac-

The End ▶

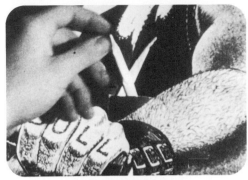

tive devil who wants to give him a free supply of drugs. In the midst of the conflict that these two arouse in Benny, he meets a hippie policeman who asks for a light for his own joint.

Then, as in many dreams, things take a turn for the worse. Images of war and death beset Benny. He is frightened of the angel, devil, and cop and tries to run away, but they run after him. Hissing bullets are heard on the sound track. Benny awakes to find himself in his apartment. In answer to a knock on the door he peers through the peephole and is confronted first by an angry Vietcong soldier and then by young ROTC trainees marching down a field. He recoils from the peephole. The final sequence shows Benny throwing up his hands in disgust, then the word "life" (taken from the magazine cover) going from misty to sharp focus, and then the words "the end" flickering on and off. This is a superficial description of Alfonso's film. Much is left out. For example, one image that really gets me is the first sight of the devil, dressed in elegant white top hat and tails, as he rises up from a row of stuffed-to-overflowing garbage cans (photographed during a New York City sanitation men's strike).

Technically speaking, this film is an editing marvel. Although it runs only ten minutes, it includes many different scenes and moments in time. Transition shots, which move the action ahead, are masterfully executed in a variety of ways: reoccurring flash frames (two or three frames that appear on the screen for a fraction of a second and are perceived almost subliminally) of the stern face of LBJ flicker ominously, as if haunting Benny; swish pans hurtle us from scene to scene; purposeful jump cuts (which condense time by implying complete actions that are not shown in entirety) reveal the tension and underlying anxiety that Benny continually seeks to escape.

◀ *The End*

SO FAR I HAVE BEEN DISCUSSING MOVIES THAT CAN BE MADE WITH direct photography. Now I will discuss *animation*. There are several kinds of animation, and I will first describe the technique made famous by Walt Disney. His drawings move and flow like natural forms in motion. Such naturalistic movement is achieved by photographing a sequence of drawings a frame at a time. The same basic scene is drawn over and over with differences so slight they are barely detectable. The thousands of individual drawings are then photographed in appropriate sequence. When the finished film is run through a projector at 24FPS, the drawings appear to move smoothly. Mr. Disney had hundreds of assistants, and I don't suggest that you attempt this time-consuming type of animation.

Some teen-agers, however, like tedious frame-by-frame photography because of the freedom it provides to invent characters and situations. A popular type of animation with teen-agers is akin to the Disney method, but instead of drawings, it involves cut paper shapes, which are moved two frames at a time on a flat background. *Circus,* which is this kind of film, was made by a sixteen-year-old named Ronnie. In *Circus* acrobats accomplish extraordinary feats, clowns do impossible acts, and animals behave like people. Ronnie drew his figures on cardboard, cut them out, and hinged their arms and legs with brads. Then he sprayed them with flat white lacquer and colored them delicately with felt-tipped markers in vivid shades. Changing their positions slightly between double-frame takes, he moved them across a gaily painted background laid on the floor. The camera, mounted on a tripod, pointed straight down at them. On screen the paper figures appear to cavort.

Peter animates twelve-inch, hard plastic, jointed mannequins, which

43

◀ *Circus*

he buys in an art store and on which he builds clay faces. For hair he uses yarn and fur. He has four or five basic bodies and converts these into an array of characters. He photographs them in what he calls "a series of experiments." His short films have no plots or titles ("titles are too important to give lightly"). It takes him sixty hours to shoot one two-and-one-half-minute experiment. Added to this is the time spent setting up lights and creating actors and sets. He shoots two frames, moves the mannequins a tiny bit, shoots two more frames, etc. On screen the figures appear to move in lifelike fashion. Sometimes he works eight to ten hours at a stretch and has no sense of time when he is so absorbed. He started out using Super 8, but now he uses a 16mm camera. Color is among the strongest ingredients for animation, and although it is more expensive, he insists on it. Instead of creating a sound track, he plays records when he shows his films. Peter feels that "you can't depend on people" and does everything except sew the costumes himself.

He was profoundly affected by *King Kong,* a famous old movie, which he first saw when he was fourteen. It combines animation with live actors. The story is of a huge gorilla which terrorizes New York City. In the scene that particularly got to Peter, King Kong scales the Empire State Building (in reality a miniature model) and grabs the heroine (a miniature dummy) through a window. Peter suddenly saw the possibility of doing the impossible, and now he does just that in all his films.

As yet Peter has not made a finished statement, so I will tell about some of his experiments. Many show heroic adventures of soldiers getting into and out of dangerous situations and frequently being killed. One memorable sequence shows some of them being swallowed in quicksand (in reality a pan of mud). Another shows men being executed by a firing squad. This was done by making a hole in each mannequin, painting on him a few drops of red paint, shooting

44

two frames, adding more paint, shooting two more frames, starting a new hole, and adding drops to the first one. After two or three hundred frames we see a group of bloody corpses.

Peter likes to set up problems and then try to solve them. How can an eight-inch monster eat a twelve-inch figure of a man? Peter used the *King Kong* method by shaping a one-inch miniature of the man in Plasticine clay and then it was easy for the larger latex-and-wire monster to devour him. When man and monster are each alone on screen, low-angle shots of the eight-inch monster lend him illusory size. Plasticine clay stays soft, so by reshaping it between takes, Peter can also make fantastic shapes appear to grow and change their looks before our very eyes. For jungle scenes he uses artificial plants and paints backdrops.

Pixilation is the application of single-frame shooting to people or to people interacting with objects. Peter used it to film an actual parade. He shot a frame or two at a time with pauses of varying lengths—a matter of seconds—in between. The marchers seem robotized on screen; he makes dolls look real and real people look like dolls. Another student used pixilation for a film in which I played a mechanical man and moved with slow, exaggerated gestures while he quickly pushed the shutter release on the camera to shoot a frame at a time with a pause in between. On screen my actions appear jolting and speeded up.

There are several nonphotographic filmmaking techniques. They offer the great advantages of being cheap and of not requiring any knowledge of photography. You don't need a camera, and you can use old or even exposed film. Another advantage is the special quality of motion and color that can only be achieved by these techniques. You won't, however, be able to create realistic images and will deal instead in simplified symbols or abstract shapes. I have seen one painted film where a daisy grew. This is about as representational as you can get because with 16mm film you are working on a frame one-quarter the size of a postage stamp. With 8mm film the frame is only one-twelfth the size of a postage stamp, so if you intend to draw or to use lettering, it is bettter to get 16mm. Anyway, don't complain if you don't have access to a camera. If there is a projector at your school, church, or community center, you can make a film with the following techniques—and without a camera.

A group of my students painted on film in art class. They took old film and washed off the emulsion (the coated surface on all film, which holds the photographic image). They used undiluted Clorox and wore rubber gloves, wiping the film with a soft cloth to expose the clear acetate, or base (synonyms for the basic plastic strip). Washed color film will turn out like washed black-and-white (B&W). The base is the same; it's the emulsion that differs. If, instead of washing unexposed film, you preserve images on already exposed film and paint over them, you see both images and paint when the movie is projected.

The art class lined up tables and made a long continuous work surface to which we fastened the film strip with masking tape. Everybody got six feet of film to paint as he chose. Some students wanted to hold an image on the screen. One girl started with a tiny dot and in each successive frame painted a slightly larger dot. After three feet of film, the dot filled the frame. For her last three feet she made the dot diminish and disappear. The effect on screen was perceived in one of two ways, either as a growing and shrinking dot or as a dot approaching and then receding from the viewer.

Another method which gives many interesting results is recommended for 8mm because the area is so limited. You paint along the strip with solid colors, stripes, diagonal strokes, or whatever, using indelible felt-tipped markers or acetate inks with brushes. On screen the colored shapes seem to flow. With both 8mm and 16mm you can also glue transparent and translucent materials onto the acetate. An extremely inventive filmmaker applied butterfly wings. Another glued photographic images from one film onto another piece of film; that is, he cut a frame from an 8mm movie and glued it onto a blank piece of 16mm film (this also works with 16mm on 16mm and 8mm on 8mm). It made a quick flash of the image on screen. For several feet of a particular action you have to cut out numerous frames of exposed film and glue them to the base.

When attaching a second layer to the film surface, you should be careful not to cover the sprocket holes by which the film is threaded onto the projector. All materials should be firmly fastened with film cement to the outside of the strip as it is wound on the reel, so that nothing tears in the film gate of the projector. I suggest that the film be sent to a laboratory as soon as possible so that the double-layered film strip (acetate plus superimposed materials) can be reproduced on a (single-layered) print. Running the piece of film you work on through the projector will sooner or later damage it because of its extra thickness.

In scratch films the animator must begin with negative B&W film that has been exposed and developed without an image so that the emulsion is preserved and the base is black, or with developed but unexposed reversal B&W film, which will also give you a black base. You need a stylus, which can be any sharp-pointed instrument, like a hatpin or compass point. The image is created by scratching through the emulsion with the stylus. As with painting, the image can be held or can flow. What appears on screen is linear rather than solid—a white line on a black background. To add color, fill in the scratched design with felt-tipped markers. If you begin with unexposed developed color film, scratching will reveal various colors, depending on how deeply toward the base you scratch; the emulsion has colored

48

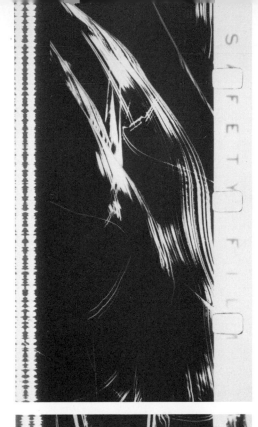

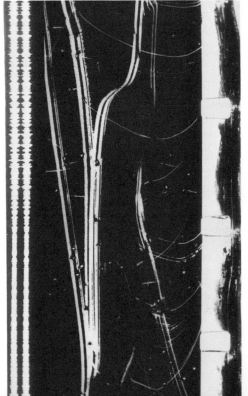

layers. You can also get unusual effects by pricking through the film with the stylus. This technique is customarily employed with others like painting and scratching. The holes can form a random pattern or can be held as a steady image. When pricking, approach from the inside of the film as it is wound on the reel, so that the raised circumference of the hole is on the outside. The shape and size of the hole can be varied slightly, depending on the stylus used.

Certain kinds of films employ any of the techniques I have described or combinations of them. For instance, when a young filmmaker chooses the lyrics of a song as his scenario or plot outline, he can use direct photography, pixilation, or nonphotographic methods. He can use people or puppets. Perhaps he will want to work with cut paper or with inanimate objects.

Josué was taken with the Beatles' song "A Day in the Life." He used direct photography and pixilation to interpret the lyrics. Hearing the Beatles' line "I'd love to turn you on," followed by lengthy electronic reverberations and no words, what pictures come to your mind? In Josué's movie, when this line is sung, a boy and girl are seen walking arm and arm; they are photographed in the conventional manner. Josué then goes into single-frame shooting and tips the couple on their sides by tilting the camera. He concludes with single-frame shots of the boy on different days in different places plus single frames of other boys' faces, which flash by so quickly that I cannot see them, although some teen-agers can. All this was done in the camera, not in editing. Two other boys made a film together using the same Beatles' song. At the phrase "I'd love to turn you on," they zoom in on a blinking automobile taillight, moving to an extreme close-up, which fills the screen with pulsating red light.

50

Alvin, when he was fifteen, made a film parody called *The Ed Skullivan Show*. He took a couple of recorded songs, built a little stage, created fantastic creatures with hand puppets, and made them mimic the singers. He played records while he filmed silently and later put the songs on a tape to be played on a tape recorder beside the projector. The final effect is very funny, especially when Alvin uses a puppet that doesn't look a bit like Aretha Franklin, plays an Aretha Franklin record, and as she really belts out a note has the puppet swallow the microphone.

Seventeen-year-old Susan combined direct photography with animation to make an amusing, subtle comment on the male-female scene without using actual people. She used both color and B&W because she could not afford to do the whole thing in color, but the result is that her film has an added expressiveness. She found her actors for *Life Is Just a Bowl of Cherries* at a fruit and vegetable stand, choosing them carefully for size, shape, and color. When a cute avocado is pursued by a parsnip, the chase is in color; Susan shot two frames, moved the vegetables slightly, shot two more, and so on (animation). She used animation again when a cabbage, which has been spinning like a top as if in excitement, is seduced by a sweet potato; this is in B&W because Susan was primarily interested in the action. To show a sliced tomato closing up, she attached a string (invisible to the camera) and had a friend pull it; at other times she kicked the table to make the vegetables move: direct photography in each case. A very resourceful girl.

José, who is twenty-three, got a late start as a filmmaker. He had been searching and had not known for what, although the things that had meant a great deal to him had invariably engaged his imagination. He has an inventive, fanciful mind and had liked the theatre so much that he had had notions of becoming an actor until he discovered filmmaking. Currently he is an assistant at FILM CLUB and also stays there at night to guard the place against theft by neighborhood junkies who might break in. *Flash* is José's first film, and it is in color. It illustrates how *special effects,* achieved through technical ingenuity, can be used to create a fantastical movie. Most of the film employs direct photography but, as you will see later, José did not restrict himself to that.

The opening scene is of a spaceship spinning past stars and planets toward earth. It lands accompanied by brilliant flashes of light, and out steps Flash, a princely-looking boy who seems somewhat dazed. We learn from the narrator that he has come from another galaxy, and although superhuman, is still a frightened, lost child. A childless woman finds Flash and takes him home with her to raise as her own son. Years later an evil man from outer space invades earth with the intention of dominating humanity. Flash, who has been leading a normal earthling's life, is challenged to subdue the enemy. He stops the intruder's rampage of destruction with a life-and-death duel. Each combatant has a special power: Flash can move at accelerated speeds while the enemy can evaporate and reappear at will. After a tense struggle, Flash defeats the invader and "the world has a new hero."

A lively imagination is one thing. Capturing it on film is another. Every time José had a fanciful idea he had to figure out how he could translate it cinematically. To show Flash's spaceship hurtling through the universe, he first glued glitter onto a large black cloth. Then he painted rubber balls to look like planets and suspended them on wires in front of the sparkling backdrop. He filmed this through a gauzy

55

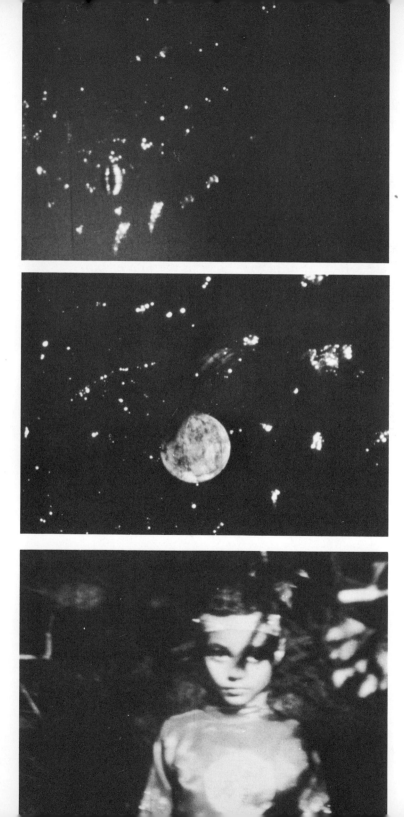

material hung in front of the camera, which gave a diffused effect to space and made the glitter twinkle. He triple-exposed the shot for greater depth: winding the film back in the camera twice, he ran it again twice to superimpose additional celestial bodies and the traveling spaceship. So that the spaceship would twirl through space, José suspended it on a piece of strong black thread, which is invisible against the black backdrop. A zoom lens moved from a wide-angle shot of the universe to a telephoto shot of the earth—a technique probably familiar to you from sports films where the zoom lens focuses first on the playing field and then zooms in to a close-up of the main action. José's camera zoomed in to give the impression of the view from a spaceship fast approaching earth. He must have spent one hundred hours on the space voyage alone. It runs about forty-five seconds on screen, and he is very happy with it.

This description of the space voyage may remind you of the movie *2001: A Space Odyssey*. You might expect that José would have seen that film but not that its director, Stanley Kubrick, would have seen *Flash*. Actually, José didn't want to watch *2001* for fear of being unduly influenced, but Mr. Kubrick did view *Flash*. He was having work done at a sound studio where technicians had volunteered to help José with special sound effects, and they screened the film for Mr. Kubrick. He was so impressed that he offered José a choice of sound effects from *2001*. Flattered and pleased, José nevertheless decided to decline the offer in favor of a movie totally his own.

Not all special effects took as much time to create as that space voyage. At one point the invader walks through the wall of a house into the living room. This was achieved with a double exposure. First exposure: the invader, costumed in white, steps out from behind a black backdrop placed in front of a black wall; the floor is also black. Second exposure: the living-room wall. The black setting does not register on the film, so the man seems to step suddenly through the

57

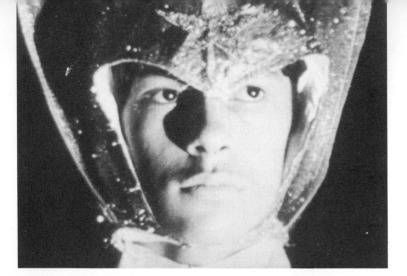

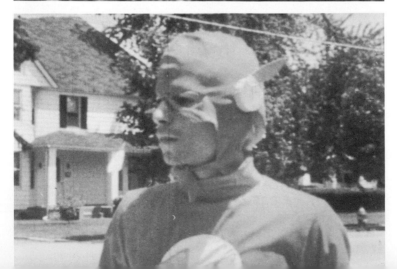

wall. I mentioned earlier that Flash has the power to move with superhuman speed. Do you remember that in the final shot of *Diana,* Diana and a little girl float in slow motion down the street? José used fast motion to accelerate Flash's actions; it was as simple as turning the knob on the camera that regulates the speed.

When the intruder invokes his power to disappear, he fades from the screen (unlike the hero of *Those Powerful Pills,* who pops off screen). This entailed photographing the actor against a black backdrop and closing the lens slowly. Closing the lens does not make the picture decrease in size; it decreases the available light. The film was then wound back in the camera, and a landscape was photographed. On screen the actor fades from the landscape. In depicting the intruder's ray gun José did two things. For some shots he scratched the film. He took a stylus and on each frame scratched tiny lines radiating outward from the gun; on screen the gun seems to be shooting rays. José also used an editing trick. After a shot of the gun firing, he spliced in a few frames of exposed but blank color reversal film. These white frames are perceived by the viewer as blinding flashes of light.

Even if he has spent thirty or forty hours on it, José does not use footage that does not meet his standards. He had wanted to show the enemy spaceship crashing into a train. For a smoke effect he had someone sifting three pounds of flour down on the train and had a fan blowing the sifted flour. It looked phony to him on screen and he discarded it. Had he filmed this in slow motion, it might have looked more convincing, but he decided the scene was unnecessary. Since José's interest was primarily in special effects, he did not give the viewer a very clear idea of the plot, so I encouraged him to have a narrator fill in details. An actor read the narration into a tape-recorder microphone while watching the film. The projector and the screen were in different rooms so that the tape recorder wouldn't pick up the

59

sound of the projector. José had the narration transferred to an optical sound track, which runs along the film print's edge where the sound is permanently lined up with the picture.

Outside my experience and acquaintanceship there are many young filmmakers. Some of their films undoubtedly resemble the ones described here. Some of the others are primarily *experimental* in that they depend on out-of-focus lights, overlapping lights and images, and designs achieved through technical maneuvering. They often dwell on such things as patterns in the snow, architectural details, and cloud formations. This kind of aesthetic stimulates some people, particularly people of a mechanical or abstract bent. They often feel that an artist's sensibility depends in part on the subtlety and sensitivity of his vision and that while producing films in which the camera concentrates on impersonal subjects, the filmmaker can express his own individuality through the relationships and juxtapositions he creates. Experimental filmmakers may also be fascinated with the machinery available for their art.

A very few of my students have made experimental films. Paul's provides a good example. Paul came to the United States from Hungary when he was eight. He brought with him buoyant optimism about the opportunities this country offers. He joined my first filmmaking workshop. When he was visiting a sound studio with me, he saw the large machine used for mixing sound and he became infatuated with it. He then got into the habit of hanging around a professional camera rental store in New York City. He studied the different kinds of lenses and other equipment. He got to know professional technicians. Because he lives in a large city where there is constant filmmaking activity, he was able to educate himself by keeping his eyes open and asking questions. In return for the information the tech-

60

nicians gladly gave him, Paul did favors for them, like carrying equipment on location.

One day, in a camera rental store, he discovered the prism lens. This has a kaleidoscope effect: the image photographed is repeated five times on the film frame. Paul just had to use that lens. He conceived a film called *Yesterday,* which is an impressionistic rendition of the yearning for friendship and love that many lonely teen-agers feel. It follows a young man who is daydreaming about a beautiful girl. We aren't sure if his visions are memories or fantasies. Paul rented the prism lens and showed the girl's face repeated five times in a single shot. The film is a collage of such technical effects.

Paul liked the freeze frame and with it showed the actor running toward the camera and suddenly freezing; on screen the movie stops and a still picture appears. This was achieved in the laboratory. Paul tied a piece of thread through the sprocket hole of the frame he wanted frozen. When that frame came up on the printing machine, the printer repeated it, printing it sixty-four times so that it would last for the amount of screen time Paul had specified (three seconds). This method only works with 16mm film because 8mm printing machines are not yet equipped to produce optical effects. If you want to do a freeze frame yourself with either 16mm or 8mm, you have to take a still camera and photograph the scene to be frozen. With your movie camera photograph an eight-by-ten-inch enlargement of the B&W still picture, keeping the film running for however long you want the frame frozen; then splice the shot into your movie. If you are working with color, shoot a color transparency (slide) and film it as it is projected from a slide projector onto a flat white matte surface.

There were several fade-ins and fade-outs in *Yesterday,* accomplished through instructions to the printer in the laboratory. You can do a fade-in in the camera by beginning a scene with the f/stop (see

page 92) closed all the way down to f/22. and, as the camera runs, opening the lens to the proper setting. A fade-out begins with the camera set at the proper f/stop, and the cameraman closes down the aperture while filming.

Paul enjoyed abstract patterns and chose locations expressly for their design possibilities (a fountain, a memorial arch, a bridge). There is a shot of the boy taken through a wrought-iron fence so that his face is framed by elaborate metalwork. Another shot shows only the boy's feet and his shadow stretching away from them. Sometimes Paul superimposes the girl's face over the boy's face, and there is a long shot of the boy on a bridge over which appears the girl's face, filling the screen as she fills his thoughts.

For Paul techniques came first and movie ideas were formed to take advantage of them. At present he is happily working at a well-paying job with a film-production company.

THERE IS A LOT TO BE SAID ABOUT VISUAL LANGUAGE OF FILM. THERE are many ways in which you communicate every day that have little to do with the spoken word. Your facial expressions, tone of voice, and gestures send messages all the time which are read by those around you. A wink, a frown, a tapping foot, can emphasize or even contradict what is said or can make a comment of its own. Similarly, "One picture is worth a thousand words." Here is a paradox: to communicate to you about visual language I must use words.

Historically, film inherited the traditions of the novel and the stage. The earliest motion pictures were called "photo plays," and the camera had a seat on the aisle. Although films have changed radically since then, many audiences and critics still tend to react to them as if they were plays or novels. This causes considerable confusion. It makes more sense to compare a movie to a dream than to drama or literature. The movie-dream originates in the filmmaker's imagination, but on screen it becomes the viewer's dream. The viewer, like the dreamer, is relatively motionless in a darkened room and is carried out of his actual location in time and space by light, movement, sound, and images. Psychologists have shown that in dreams symbolic language can reveal our emotions, attitudes, and experiences without rational restraint. Films can do much the same thing. The viewer, without blinking an eye, can be transported from one place to another and watch scenes unfold from high up in the air or from under the earth, through a wall or through another person's eyes; logic and rationality can be utterly ignored. There is such freedom here that it is beyond words.

When I leave a theatre, I am suspicious of people in the lobby talking a mile a minute about their reactions. Have they really let

the film in or have they held it away, using their intellects as walls between them and the film experience? My verbal response to a film takes hours, days, or weeks to form. Some people argue that not to talk about what a film—your own or someone else's—means to you is to avoid full understanding.

Many students are introduced to teen-age filmmaking by looking at movies made by other students. Frequently they don't have anything to say immediately afterward. Months later, while working on their own productions, they will refer to things they saw at that first screening. They carry those films around in their heads, and the impact only becomes apparent gradually.

Each art form has its own language. You may not be able to talk about a novel with ease, or about a poem or painting or piece of sculpture; music or dance may leave you speechless. How do you know when you have been reached if you cannot put your interpretation into words? I cannot give you any pat answers, but I will share my observations with you. Knowledge and understanding bring with them a feeling of coherence with yourself. Ignorance and misunderstanding are characterized by uneasiness and confusion, though this is not to be mixed up with the anxiety that comes from knowing but not liking what you know. So many things are shown on screen that are distasteful or disturbing. Andy Warhol, who is a leading force in underground films, depicts people in grievous circumstances, but viewers are often exhilarated by the way they are revealed. Although he is using characters who border on being freaks, he exposes common human dilemmas. People who do not understand his movies are frequently offended, angered, or bored by them. Your response to any given film depends largely on the quality and breadth of imagination and experience you are able and willing to bring to it.

Did you realize that only two of the films I have described had verbal sound tracks? While watching the other films, few viewers notice that they are wordless. It must be that the pictures are sufficiently expressive. The filmmakers themselves never seem to mind that they do not have talking pictures. Admittedly, as an amateur filmmaker becomes professional and his skills increase, he usually wants a sound track with words. Sounds and words can become an important part of the total film experience. For the beginning filmmaker, however, dialogue is not essential.

How, then, do you read film? You pay attention to place, action, faces, gestures, postures, movements, significant objects, the quality of photography and editing, nuances in B&W, and choices of color. Jesus (who made *An Unpleasant Evening*) has a fine instinct for what is visually significant, as is evident in his third film, *A Park Called Forsyth*. It shows an encounter on the Lower East Side in New York, which erupts into a teen-age gang fight. While the film is a nostalgic look at the gangs that have now passed into folklore and myth, it also demonstrates how boredom can lead to gratuitous violence. Jesus did not think of himself as being nostalgic or romantic about his subject; he was not consciously commenting on the fact that gangs have disappeared from his neighborhood; he was not making a point about aimlessness as a motivation for violent behavior. He was telling a story with pictures.

Many viewers, I'm sorry to say, do not look beyond the surface of this movie. They see only its obvious melodrama and not what Jesus is saying. In his films, Jesus deals with loneliness and identity and the way people cope. How does he tell us that gang members are very much concerned with their identities? In the opening shots he shows empty Forsyth Park, a park made of stone, concrete, and a few scraggly trees. On every wall the boys have written their names close together, as if admitting that each one feels like nothing alone but that together they achieve a sense of identity. Among the scrawled

67

signatures we see the words *A Park Called Forsyth, a film by Jesus Cruz*. It seems that the boys, by writing their names, are trying to make a mark on the world, and Jesus, by doing his screen credits as graffiti, is identifying with those boys' plight. From the graffiti the camera moves to the park swings, which are empty and swaying slightly. The effect was calculated; Jesus pushed the swings before photographing them. The image is strong: an aura of loneliness and abandonment pervades. The tenor of the movie has been established.

A group of boys enters the park. Nothing happens. Viewers may begin to squirm but that's all right. It is important that we see the boys doing nothing and feel their aimlessness. They are as fascinating as a flock of pigeons. As they perch on a bench, one fellow emerges as leader. We recognize this because he pushes the others aside and roosts highest up on the back of the bench, which thus becomes a ritualistic throne. A boy and girl, obviously absorbed in each other, enter the park. The viewer knows trouble is in store because the camera cuts swiftly back and forth between the approaching couple, strolling with arms entwined, and the watching gang, looking meaner and meaner. As the couple passes by, the gang pounces on the boy and roughs him up. Their own boredom and resentment have found relief in action against a boy who is enjoying himself and who seems to have a sense of his individual identity. We gather from the gang leader's strutting walk and attentive gaze that he wanted to impress the girl. When he triumphantly approaches her, she looks furious, scratches at him, then flees with her boyfriend. The gang settles back on the bench as if nothing has happened. The group convulsion has passed.

The boy who was attacked returns with his own gang, bent on revenge. They chase the first group into an alley, and a vicious fight ensues. The boy we saw with his girl friend turns out to be the leader of the second gang. He has been wearing a bicycle chain around his

neck as an ornament. It becomes the weapon with which he strangles the other gang leader, whose body falls to the pavement. He looks dead. The other boys do not see this confrontation because they are busy fighting one another. When they become aware of the lifeless body, the action freezes for an instant. Then they run away, except for one boy who stands spellbound beside the corpse. Snapping out of it, he rips off the handkerchief he had wound around his knuckles and flings it at the body. He, too, runs away.

Jesus thinks very effectively in images. The alley was the first one that occurred to him. When he told me that alley would be in his next film, I asked, "What's it going to be about?" His answer was, "I don't know, but that alley is in it." In the finished production the alley does not appear until the last scene. It is a dead end, and its walls convey the compression of the boys' emotional lives—they constantly feel squeezed. The second image that rose to his consciousness was the graffiti-scrawled wall, and after that Jesus filled in the story of his movie.

As I keep repeating, film images convey much more than plot. Jesus transforms objects visually from one thing to another and so makes multileveled comments. When the gang of boys first alights on the park bench and the leader sits above his friends, the bench suddenly suggests a throne and we have a glimpse of the boys' fantasy lives. The boy who first appears with the girl is wearing a bicycle chain as a necklace; later he commits murder with it. A bike chain is a common object used to lock a bike against theft. Jesus has the boy transform it into an article of personal adornment, and so gives us information about the boy's concept of his masculinity and in a general way about what sort of life he leads. As the boy strangles his enemy with that chain, we are shocked into realizing something about the relationship between appearances and reality. Perhaps we even

73

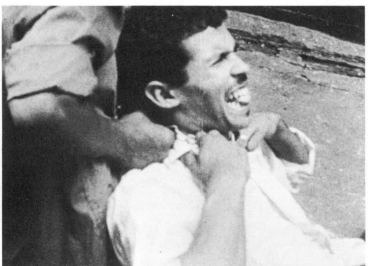

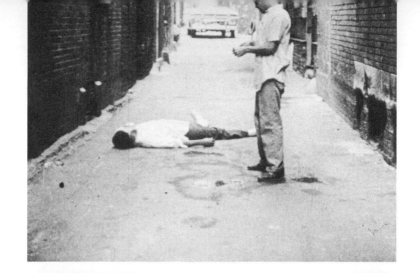

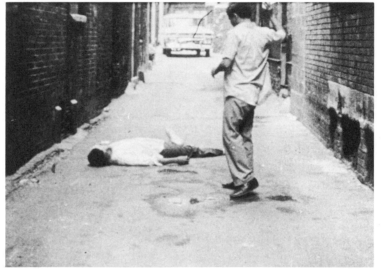

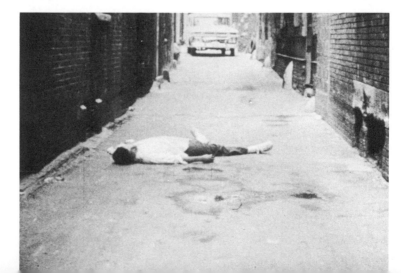

feel how dangerous it is to assume we know what a bike chain—or a boy—is capable of.

Jesus invests himself in his films. Part of him is in each person in *A Park Called Forsyth,* just as part of a dreamer is in each character he dreams. This seems particularly true in the final scene when one gang member remains in the alley, staring ambivalently at the corpse, then removes the handkerchief from his knuckles and flings it at the corpse and dashes off, as if to say, I reject you and your actions. The dead leader represents impulsive, reckless, thoughtless behavior, which leads to self-destruction; the observer in Jesus studies the leader, too, and rejects him.

There is thematic consistency in the work of every filmmaker. In all of Jesus' films we meet people who are lonely, who cannot relate positively to one another, and who are troubled by violent impulses. In his first film, *The Loser,* a boy accidentally kills a girl at a party, and he and all the guests abandon her body. In *An Unpleasant Evening* Ivan draws a knife and is about to attack Chicky with it but is restrained by a friend. No matter what the plots or settings of his movies, Jesus will continue to weave into them his personal concerns. As his own feelings are modified by time, maturity, and experience, his films will change but only so far as he himself changes.

Is it any wonder that many artists do not like to talk about their finished works? It's a little bit like telling someone a story and then being asked to tell it again in different words. You feel that your listener was not paying attention the first time. If talking brought adequate satisfaction to artists, as it does to many people, they would not need another form of communication. What medium they choose depends on how they are best able to express who they are and what they see.

In large commercial pictures the situation is quite different from the one I have been describing. Where millions of dollars are involved in the employment of thousands of people, the industry has come to feel that it cannot afford to run the risk of a creative director dominating the film. Films are produced to outdo each other in attracting The Audience, as if we were a single, mindless mass, whose responses and attitudes are codifiable. Obviously, the formulas work for enticing and entertaining people. But by removing films so far from the unique creativity of an individual filmmaker, Hollywood fails to recognize viewers' capacities for response to serious works.

"Communication" and "self-expression" are overworked words in describing the value and purpose of creative filmmaking. The young filmmaker is more interested in relating to himself than in addressing any future group of people who might see his movie. The audience is very remote to him during creation and production. When his film is finished, he hopes people will like it. He is not particularly eager to have his work analyzed and dissected. He wants the audience to accept his film and through it to accept him. He does not want primarily to enlighten or impress or entertain others, since his motivating concern is with himself. His audiences will respond to his film to the extent that their imaginative capacities and his experiences touch, and he can only hope that he and they will find a common meeting ground.

The Movie Camera. AS JOSUÉ HELD A MOVIE CAMERA FOR THE FIRST time, he said, "I want to know everything about it. What makes it tick?" Other students haven't cared to learn any more about how and why a camera works than is necessary to get images onto the movie screen more or less as they originally envision them. Everyone needs to understand how to load film into his camera and how a satisfactory picture is achieved. For the benefit of those who want to know more, I will go into some detail.

All the way from the old 8mm windup camera, used by your proud parents to record your babyhood and high points of family history, to the latest 70mm Hollywood machine, basic camera functioning remains the same. All motion-picture cameras photograph in rapid succession a series of still pictures. When these stills are projected at a very fast rate, they seem to move. Just as the shutter in the camera closes while the next frame to be exposed is pulled into place, so the shutter in the projector must close, causing the screen to go dark until the next still picture can be projected. The screen is totally darkened for half of the total length of the movie; the viewer is not consciously aware of blackouts because the picture preceding each one is still being perceived by him after it has left the screen, due to the visual phenomenon known as "persistence of vision." If black intermissions did not occur in projection, images would pour down the screen and be perceived as an unintelligible blur. Psychologically we bring our own perceptive capacities to a movie, and this gives the viewing experience vitality; physiologically we automatically contribute persistence of vision, and this makes the series of stills come to life.

A movie camera works exactly like a still camera, except that it takes many, many stills. The pictures have not the slightest motion, yet the sense of motion is totally convincing as sixteen to twenty-four separate still pictures are projected each second; because there is an equal number of blackouts, the eye receives up to forty-eight individual signals every second.

In movie cameras a loading spool feeds off unexposed film to a take-up spool, which receives exposed footage. The film has sprocket holes, or perforations, along one edge, which catch on the sprocket wheel or claws, insuring that the film proceeds smoothly past the lens and that one frame at a time is exposed. A motor turns the take-up spool and opens and closes the shutter. This motor may be activated by a spring, in which case it is rewound by hand after each filming sequence; it may be electrically driven by batteries, or it may have a cord that plugs into an ordinary electrical outlet. The shutter is located in the aperture, or opening, just behind the lens. When the shutter opens, the lens registers the image on the film's light-sensitive emulsion coating. Then the shutter closes, and the next frame is pulled into position ready to be exposed. Later in the photo laboratory the images are developed on the film strip.

The cameraman sees the scene to be photographed through the viewfinder of the camera. There are two designs. With a reflex viewer the cameraman looks through the same lens used in exposing the film. With a parallax viewer he looks through a separate lens, which approximates the view through the filming lens. Reflex viewing is considered preferable, since it captures exactly the scene that is being filmed; furthermore, if the lens is not in focus, it will be immediately apparent in a reflex viewer. In an extreme close-up a parallax viewer will not accurately frame the object being photographed unless parallax correction is built into the viewfinder (as it frequently is) to compensate for the difference between the viewfinding lens and the filming lens.

All cameras have a shutter release, which activates the camera motor and sends the film from the loading spool to the take-up spool. Shutter releases often have three positions:

1. Continuous run, which stops when the cameraman lifts his finger.
2. Locked continuous run, which enables the cameraman to walk away from the camera while it is running (this is particularly useful if the cameraman wishes to appear in the film).
3. Single-frame shooting, which takes a single picture with a push of the release (necessary for pixilation and animation).

Many cameras have adjustable shutter speeds, ranging from 8FPS to 64FPS. Such flexibility permits fast- and slow-motion effects during projection. Projectors run at fixed speeds. A 16mm sound projector, for example, projects at 24FPS. If the camera filmed the action at 24FPS, the action will appear to take the same length of time on screen as it did in front of the camera. If, however, the camera was filming the action at 12FPS (fast motion), it will unfold at twice that speed on the screen because the projector turns out a relentless 24FPS. Filming the action at 64FPS (slow motion) will make the screen time two and one half times slower than it actually was, for the projector will only take 24FPS.

In all filmmaking you must decide whether to put the camera on a tripod or to hold it. Picture steadiness is a requirement that some audiences make of a movie; they complain of nausea if the entire film looks as though an earthquake were in progress. Yet a tripod does not guarantee viewer comfort. I have seen footage shot from a camera firmly mounted on a tripod in which all the walls tilted at an eighty-degree angle and gave the uneasy impression of an ocean liner about to sink. The question is not whether or not to use a tripod for its own sake. You should consider what method best suits the particular scene being shot. Sometimes a tripod is called for, at other times a pistol grip, and at still others a hand-held shot will be most effective. To hold the heavier 16mm camera takes more support (or muscle) than to hold a smaller camera.

Alfonso prides himself on being the "human tripod." He means he can hold the camera almost as firmly as a tripod can; he pivots from the waist when he needs to pan. Young filmmakers often feel that a tripod is inhibiting. Each beginner will have to discover what approach he likes best, keeping in mind that the picture seen in the viewfinder will be magnified hundreds of times on screen, as will the camera's movements.

In some filming situations a tripod is always or almost always recommended:

1. Telephoto filming needs a steady camera because the slightest movement is tremendously magnified.
2. Extreme long shots which encompass an entire landscape look unnaturally shaky if there is camera movement.
3. For a smooth pan that encompasses more than ninety degrees a tripod helps.
4. Titling often requires a steady, fixed camera so that the letters do not jounce.
5. Animation and some pixilation require a tripod.
6. A tripod is absolutely essential for making characters or objects disappear by popping them out of the frame.

8mm, Super 8, and 16mm: Some Comparisons. THERE ARE MANY
movie cameras on the market, and when you add to these cameras
those that are no longer manufactured but are tucked away in closets
and attics, you can realize that it would be impossible to describe
each of them fully here. I will mention some differences for compari-
son. Most people are able at least to borrow a camera. Whatever
is available to you will predetermine or limit your choice. The 35mm
and 70mm are completely impractical for the filmmaker working on
as little money as possible. Even if you were presented with one
of these stupendous cameras as a gift, you would go broke paying for
film and processing.

The 8mm has been around for twenty-five years. It was designed for the home-movie market and replaced the original 16mm amateur movie equipment of the 1930's. Cameras and projectors for Regular 8 (as it is now called) are no longer being manufactured because the industry converted to Super 8 in 1966. Film stock and processing for Regular 8 will nevertheless be available for some years to come.

8mm film measures a good quarter inch in width (precisely: 8mm in width) and projects at 16FPS. Most cameras use a twenty-five-foot spool of 16mm film, which runs through the camera once, is flipped over by the cameraman, and runs again, exposing half the width each time. After processing in the laboratory, the film is slit in two and is returned to you on a fifty-foot reel, giving a screen time of five minutes. Some cameras use a spool and others a cartridge. Be sure you know which your camera takes when ordering film. With a spool you thread the film manually; with a cartridge threading is automatic and so error free. Some 8's have spring-wind motors and others are battery driven. Later models have automatic exposure meters but many require the cameraman to use a light meter.

The Super 8 camera is a recent innovation and incorporates all the advances developed over the past twenty years in the 8mm field. While the film gauge (width) is the same for both, the picture area is greater with Super 8 than with Regular 8 because the sprocket holes are much smaller (as well they should be on such a narrow strip). Super 8 projects at 18FPS rather than 16FPS. The new film is not interchangeable with Regular 8, nor can it be shown on Regular 8 projectors. The more elaborate of the new 8 projectors can accommodate both Regular and Super 8 prints.

Everything about Super 8 has been designed to reduce the chance of error and make filming as easy, pleasant, and uncomplicated as possible. The film now comes in fifty-foot magazine-loading cartridges, which eliminate manual threading. An automatic light meter and battery-driven motor are standard features on even the most inexpensive of these cameras. The development of sound on film never got very far in Regular 8, but we can anticipate important progress in Super 8 sound tracks; sound on film will play an increasingly large part in filmmaking with 8.

The 16mm camera appears to be a giant when compared with 8. Originally it was designed to provide a more accessible means of filmmaking than had been possible in 35mm (a wide film strip necessitates large equipment). It has become, on the whole, a very professional machine and is preferred for television, educational, and industrial films. The fact that the 16mm film gauge is exactly twice that of 8 is the most important distinction between them. Film and processing costs are about double, too, which may be discouraging to the potential purchaser.

Students grasp the mechanics in one or two sessions. The less expensive 16mm cameras have spring-wind motors, which drive seventeen to forty feet of film on one wind; then you have to stop and rewind it. Projection speed is 24FPS; seven and one-half inches of film pass the camera aperture every second (a one-hundred-foot spool gives three minutes of screen time). Few of these cameras have automatic light meters, and parallax viewfinders are common on older models.

The life expectancy of a 16mm camera is twenty to thirty years, so a second-, third-, or even fourth-hand machine can work very well. Some older models use a fifty-foot magazine load (from the days when 16mm was for amateurs), but I recommend one-hundred-foot loading spool models because processing on the fifty-foot magazine costs the same as on the one-hundred-foot spools. Another drawback of very old 16mm cameras is that they film at 16FPS. While most current 16mm projectors have a speed of 16FPS for silent films, they can project a film with an optical sound track only at 24FPS; to allow yourself the possibility of adding such a sound track to your

86

film, you must shoot it at 24FPS. Furthermore, to be broadcast on television, a film must be shot at 24FPS. In blowing up 8mm to 16mm the original film must have been exposed at 24FPS; 16mm is required when showing a film on television or in a theatre equipped for professional movies. 16mm demands more attention to details from the cameraman and in so doing gives more satisfaction.

An 8mm camera weighs under four pounds, and a 16mm camera weighs six to twenty-five pounds. A good sturdy tripod is especially helpful with the heavier cameras, although many students prefer to use a shoulder brace or pistol grip; hand-held shots can work very well, too. Some students have used their fathers' Regular 8's to start with (the very cameras that their fathers had used to photograph them as children). These first 8mm experiences often prove to teen-agers (and their parents) that as young filmmakers they have a real talent and sustained interest. Parents will sometimes then provide a 16mm machine.

The path to the 16mm equipment, or any film equipment for that matter, is often through a movie club at your school or community center. Sometimes a group of close friends with moviemaking in mind can pool their money and set up their own filmmaker's cooperative. For a group of five or six members one camera is all that is needed because the actual shooting of the film represents the smallest amount of time in the entire production.

A final suggestion on the how-to aspects of camera functioning: get the manufacturer's instruction booklet. Usually a camera's original owner throws this booklet away. When second-hand equipment provides the way for you to begin, write to the manufacturer of the camera you plan to use. Ask for the manual, clearly specifying all model numbers. They will most likely send you the instructions even for cameras they no longer make. All camera companies have a consumer-service division, which is there just for such requests.

Film Stocks. BEFORE IT HAS BEEN EXPOSED OR DEVELOPED, FILM IS called raw stock. The base of the film is composed of a clear acetate material. The composition of light-sensitive particles that coats the base is called emulsion. There are dozens of raw stocks to choose from. Besides the obvious difference between color and B&W stock, there is another important factor to be noted. When you think of film, you must think of light. The kind of illumination you plan to use (artificial light and/or sunlight) will affect your choice of raw stock. The intensity of light must be taken into account, too. Each film is designed to record images with a precise amount of light; too much will cause the picture to overexpose, too little will cause it to underexpose. A standard for films' sensitivity to light has been generally adopted by film manufacturers under the American Standards Association (ASA) ratings.

The higher the ASA number, the more sensitive the film to light. This means that a film like Kodak 4X ASA 400, designed for low-light situations, would be overexposed in bright sunlight. Every film has two ASA ratings. With B&W the variations in ASA on the same film are due to varying light intensity. For example, if you use Plus-X, designed for bright light, in daylight the ASA is 50, but if you use it with tungsten light, the ASA is 40. Artificial light, though seemingly blinding at times, is not as intense as sunlight. With color there are two ASA ratings for each film type, one to apply when a filter is used, and one to apply when it is not.

A correction filter (*e.g.,* Wratten #85) is necessary when using a color film that was balanced for tungsten light (*e.g.,* Photoflood 3200K) with natural light. Film balanced for daylight will need a filter (*e.g.,* Wratten #80B) when it is used indoors with tungsten light. A filter cuts down the amount of light striking the film. This accounts for the markedly different ASA scales listed for any given type of color film: the ASA number is determined by the amount and intensity of light and whether or not a filter is to be used.

All raw stock for 8mm is reversal type. In 16mm both reversal and negative types are available. Film registers the image in a negative fashion. White objects register as black, red ones as green, etc. With reversal, the film that goes through the camera has its negative image reversed in the. developing process so that white objects will appear as white on the original and red ones will appear as red. With negative, white objects still appear black and red ones still appear green after the film is developed. Original reversal may be projected on the screen, whereas a print must be made from negative original before it will project the true color of the subject. 8mm and Super 8mm do not come in negative and 16mm negative involves a work print, which is too costly for most beginning filmmakers. For a partial list of American reversal film stocks to consider before buying, see list on pages 100-101.

The choice of color or B&W may present an artistic decision or an economic reality. Recently one teen-ager said when he had planned his script, "Color has no meaning in my film. I want it to be all gray." Regular 8 filmmakers will discover that color film is less expensive than B&W because the sales volume in color film is much greater than in B&W. In Super 8 prices are nearly the same. Color in 16mm, however, doubles the cost of stock, processing, and prints. Again economic considerations may predetermine your choices.

Have all your film developed at a laboratory to avoid getting bogged down in the slow, boring business of developing. In still photography there are rarely more than thirty-six pictures on a roll; an important part of the creation depends on the photographer's skill in developing and printing his film. This is not true in developing and printing movie films where the lengthy spool of film requires highly complicated procedures. If you do develop your own films (for kicks or for economy), you still won't be able to make your own prints. Why not save your time and energy for more interesting and rewarding tasks?

You can ask the clerk who sells you film where to have it processed. Unless there is a film-processing laboratory near you, you will have to rely on the mails. There are mail-order houses that sell and process film less expensively than smaller outfits because they do a large volume of business; they advertise in photography magazines and will send you a free catalogue upon request.

The Camera Lens. EVERY LENS HAS AN APERTURE, WHICH FUNC-
tions rather like the pupil of the eye. For film to be exposed correctly
when light on the photographic subject is dim, the lens aperture must
be wide open, just as the pupil must be wide open in dim light to
enable us to see. As light intensity on the subject increases, the aperture size decreases; so does the pupil. To carry the analogy further,
our optic nerve system has a limited tolerance to intense light; recall
that each type of film has its own level of light tolerance, which is
recorded in its ASA rating. The lens diaphragm can be compared to
the iris of the eye. It surrounds the aperture and increases in size
when the aperture decreases and decreases when the aperture increases. The f/stops indicate the size of the aperture. By choosing the
correct f/stop when you set the lens diaphragm you adjust available
light to film sensitivity. The f/stop markings, ranging in some cases
from f/1.4 (biggest diaphragm opening) to f/22. (smallest opening), are found on the outer rim of the lens. You can set the lens
properly if you take a reading on a light meter of the subject light
intensity.

An equally important aspect of the lens is its focus. Some lenses
have a fixed focus, which means that all subjects being photographed
are in focus from approximately four feet to infinity (the symbol for
infinity, ∞, looks like a figure eight lying on its side). The drawback
of fixed-focus lenses is that nothing in the picture is precisely sharp
and everything is only relatively clear. Furthermore, the fixed-focus
lens does not allow for depth of field variations whereby close objects
appear to be in sharp focus while distant subjects appear soft or
totally out of focus.

Better lenses allow for critical focus. With them, however, the

93

cameraman needs to be aware of depth of field qualities. He must know that if the camera is taking a tracking shot (moving toward the subject) a follow (changing) focus will be necessary to keep the object being photographed sharp, and it will also be called for when the camera is stationary and the subject is moving either closer to or farther away from it.

There is a strange and interesting phenomenon that I can best describe with the axiom: (1) The larger the f/stop, the shallower the depth of field. (2) The smaller the f/stop, the greater the depth of field. At f/1.4 with the lens set at six feet, objects at five and one-half feet will appear fuzzy, and so will objects at six and one-half feet. Objects at ten feet will be totally out of focus. If you leave the focus set at six feet and close the f/stop down to f/22., objects will be in focus from three feet to ∞.

There are four basic lenses: wide angle, normal, telephoto, and zoom. A wide-angle lens allows the cameraman to take in a much wider area than the human eye can see when staring straight ahead; as the lens widens the perspective, it creates a depth distortion, which makes objects appear to be farther away from the camera than they really are. A normal lens records approximately the same range as the human eye. A telephoto lens magnifies distant objects, bringing them extremely close; this foreshortens distances. A zoom lens combines the attributes of the other three; it can do what each of them can do and in addition it can move between wide angle, normal, and telephoto during filming. A turret is mounted on many camera models. It has two or three openings into which various lenses can be fitted. One note of caution: When arranging lenses in a three-hole turret, always place the telephoto lens farthest from the wide-angle lens; you may even have to remove it when using wide angle because the wide angle may photograph the long snout of the telephoto lens.

Treat your lens kindly, for it is the key to picture quality. Never

94

clean a lens with dry tissue because you will rub in dust particles which may cause tiny scratches. The safest cleaning procedure is to brush or blow off loose dust, dampen the lens surface with lens-cleaning solution, and wipe it with a solution-dampened tissue. Avoid getting fingerprints on the lens because acidic oils will permanently etch the coating on the lens. Clean fingerprints off at once with solution-dampened tissue.

The Light Meter. WITH THE "ELECTRIC EYE" METER, WHICH IS built into some cameras, the f/stop diaphragm automatically adjusts to the correct opening if it has the proper information. It needs to know the shutter speed (how long will the shutter remain open to expose each frame of film?) and the film's sensitivity to light (its ASA). Then, as the lens takes in light, its diaphragm adjusts to the correct diameter. A tiny battery supplies power for this operation.

If the meter is a separate unit, the cameraman must read the light intensity and manually adjust the lens diaphragm's f/stop. There is nothing complicated about light meters, although they can look mysterious to the person who has never used one. There are two designs. Reflected light meters, which are most common, are available for very little money. Incident light meters represent more of an investment. An incident meter reads the light as it falls on the subject, whereas a reflected meter receives light as it bounces off the subject. Some meters can be used in either way; they are convertible. Considering the cost, let's concern ourselves with the reflected meter.

Here is the usual procedure for determining the proper f/stop.

1. Set the meter's ASA scale to that of the film in the camera.
2. Point the meter directly, holding it six to eight inches from the surface of the subject. Take care not to block the light falling on the subject with your body or hand.
3. Note the light intensity being indicated on the meter by a delicate needle.
4. Set the shutter speed (indicated on the meter as *sec.*, for "seconds") as dictated by the light-intensity reading.
5. The corresponding f/stop will appear next to the shutter speed, *e.g.*, 1/50 sec. at f/11.

The formula is: ASA plus light intensity plus shutter speed equals correct f/stop.

Be sure to study the instruction manual for your particular light meter because each model operates differently. If your meter is second-hand, obtain the booklet from the manufacturer.

Lights. YOUNG FILMMAKERS TEND TO USE AVAILABLE LIGHT WHEN-ever possible. Ordinarily they do not like to be bothered with mounting photoflood lamps. With the advent of high-speed films it has become possible to use natural-light sources more than ever before, but there will be occasions when tungsten (artificial) light will be required. With B&W film any kind of light will work as long as it is of adequate intensity (let your light meter be your guide).

When using color film, follow the film manufacturer's recommendations carefully in selecting the appropriate lamp. The easiest and most popular source for lighting interiors is the sun gun. (Don't handle the glass part of this lamp because skin oils rub off and shorten its life.) It is designed to be held by hand or clamped to a light stand, door, chair, or other convenient object. An alternative is the photoflood lamp which is shaped like a regular light bulb and must be screwed into a socket that has been mounted on an aluminum reflector. These sockets are available with metal clamps attached so that they, too, can be hung wherever they are needed. Another possibility is the reflected photoflood bulb. It has a built-in reflector because part of its interior is painted silver, and it can be used in existing light fixtures on location.

When a filmmaker gets into artificial lighting, he is surprised by how much time it takes to light a scene. He needs extension cords, adequate electrical outlets, and, to prevent harsh hot spots and severe shadows, a bare minimum of two lights. It is a good idea to pack a suitcase with all your electrical paraphernalia, taking special care to wrap lamps in soft padding. Get everything set up before your actors arrive. You may find it helpful to have an assistant in charge of lighting. Arranging lights takes a lot of time and energy; they get extremely hot and cannot be touched until they have cooled off; and they seem to have a high rate of breakage by accident.

Some Suggested American Reversal Film Stocks

CAMERA	FILM	ASA FOR DAYLIGHT	ASA FOR TUNGSTEN LIGHT
	Kodak B&W Stocks		
S8, 16	Kodak Plus-X This is a fine grain film especially designed for outdoor use when there is bright light.	50	40
S8, 16	Kodak Tri-X A moderately fast film used most frequently indoors with some photo illumination.	200	160
16	Kodak 4-X Best for night photography or indoors where there is little illumination. Image is grainy. Can be used in brilliant sunlight with neutral density filter.	400	320
	Comparable B&W Stocks from DuPont		
R8,* 16	Rapid Reversal 930A	64	50
R8,* 16	High Speed Reversal 931A	160	125
R8,* 16	High Speed Rapid Reversal 932A	320	250
R8,* 16	Ultra High Speed Rapid Reversal 933A	500	400
	Kodak Color Stocks		
R8, 16	Kodachrome II Daylight film A fine grain film especially designed for outdoor use when there is sufficient light. A Wratten #80B filter must be used with photoflood lights or the color will appear unnaturally orange-yellow (because daylight is much bluer than artificial light).	25	12 (with #80B filter)

Format	Film and description	(with #85 filter)	(no filter)
8, R8, 16	**Kodachrome II** *(top of row cut off)*	*(cut)*	*(cut)*
S8	**Type A** Designed especially for Super 8 cameras that have #85 filter built in. Color balanced for photoflood lights. Using outdoors without filter results in unnaturally blue-green light.	100 (with #85 filter)	125 (no filter)
S8	**Super Kodachrome** Designed for Super 8 only. High-speed color for indoor use with photoflood lights. May be used outdoors with #85 filter, but not recommended if you can use Kodachrome II Type A.	16 (with #85 filter)	25 (no filter)
16	**Ektachrome Commercial 7255** Makes excellent release prints but is not designed for projection of the original. Outdoor use.	80 (with #85 filter)	125 (no filter)
16	**Ektachrome EF 7242** Makes excellent release prints but is not designed for projection of the original. Indoor use. If prints are not planned, use Kodachrome II, which has beautiful color in the original but loses in the prints.		
	Comparable Color Stocks from Ansco		
16	GAF Anscochrome D/50	50	25 (with #80B filter)
16	GAF Anscochrome D/100	100	50 (with #80B filter)
16	GAF Anscochrome D/200	200	100 (with #80B filter)

* Regular 8 B&W is very difficult to obtain at local photo shops. There is a mail-order department at Kin-O-Lux, Inc., 17 West 45th Street, New York, N. Y. 10036, from which you can order Regular 8 B&W. Processing is included in their purchase price. They also make good Regular 8 and Super 8 prints in B&W or color. They will send you a catalogue upon request.

WHAT DOES THE YOUNG FILMMAKER PUT ON PAPER PRIOR TO AC-
tual filming? Everything from neatly typewritten and detailed de-
scriptions of the movie to a few hieroglyphics scribbled hastily. It
would be rather foolish to sit down before a blank piece of paper and
think, now what am I going to make my movie about? Remember,
Jesus started with two images, the alley and the graffiti-scrawled wall,
and the rest of *A Park Called Forsyth* followed from these. There are
several other ways that your movie may begin to take form in your
mind. John Earl was plagued by an unhappy personal experience he
had had four years earlier. Murray's starting point was his affection
for and fascination with his grandmother. Long before Susan became
interested in film she had been intrigued by fruits and vegetables and
had enjoyed sketching and painting them.

Let's assume that you know what your film is going to be about.
What then? For *A Park Called Forsyth* Jesus wrote out his story in
a very nice hand, describing only the action. In professional jargon
this kind of script is called a treatment. Nuances and subtleties are
not included. Jesus felt secure enough knowing he had the basic
structure firmly down on paper. Invariably Jesus loses his treatment
after a few days of filming, and none is known to survive.

John Earl and his group carefully plotted out each shot before they
began to film, so that the movie was fully created on paper in a shooting script. While this approach may rob the finished movie of a
certain spontaneity, there is much to be said for it. They were so
well organized that they shot the whole thing in one day. In their
shooting script each scene was fully described with most nuances and
subtleties explicit. Camera positions (close-up, reverse angle, cut,
fade-out) were clearly indicated. Even the editing was preplanned

103

(cut to exterior, dissolve to close-up). Traditionally this method is employed in large productions with many specialists working together. The team needs to be aware of what is going on. When a movie is the work of one person, such a detailed script is less important.

In a documentary you cannot have a shooting script. Murray used a simple treatment when photographing his grandmother. Susan did not use any script. Her central theme had to be devised after she had assembled the vegetables and discovered what would work. An urge, not even an idea, compelled her to improvise spontaneously as she filmed. Movies that make use of nonphotographic techniques like punching and gluing do not require a script, either.

Between 1915 and 1926, D. W. Griffith made some of the most lavish films ever created. They employed casts of thousands. He never put a word on paper in the early years. It was all in his head. He was fantastically central: he did his own editing and directing, designed sets and costumes, created the story, cast actors, and made titles. His films had no sound tracks, but at each performance in large theatres full symphony orchestras played the music he scored. In smaller theatres his score was played on the piano. As he traveled around to various cities for premieres of his latest movies he did further cutting so that no two prints of his early films are alike. He was a genius who never felt a film was finished. He demonstrated that an individualist can devise his own approach to getting ideas on film.

Jaime Barrios, the present teacher at FILM CLUB, discovered this for himself. He has, at twenty-three, been making movies for eight years. In the beginning, in his native Chile, his films had elaborate stories. Today they do not, and he uses no scripts. For Jaime, making a film is like playing jazz. He improvises. As a jazz musician must know the scale and chord structures without thinking about them, a filmmaker must be in control of basic film elements. He can then utilize them in complicated ways (as does the musician with scales

104

and chords). Jaime says, "You zoom or pan as you react spontaneously to the subject. A chord may have only three notes, but these can be used in thousands of combinations and tempos." He does not stop to think what he is doing. He feels like the leader of a jazz group who has developed a high degree of rapport with his company through close association with them.

Instead of planning ahead, Jaime ferrets out his original vision (as jazz players keep in mind the melody) from what is happening in front of his camera. He does not use actors. He extracts from people who are portraying themselves the qualities that express his point of view. I call this commentary film because it is more subjective than a documentary. Jaime believes that "this approach requires motor-driven, magazine-load synchronous sound equipment—and a good sound man." As you can see, his method is best suited to advanced filmmakers.

At seventeen L. C. could not write, but he was gifted at sketching and drawing. He had never heard of a storyboard (comic-strip-like drawings of the movie plot), but that is in effect what he made. Perhaps he was subconsciously influenced by his enthusiasm for comic books. Throughout the entire shooting he clutched that drawing, referring to it often. In Hollywood a storyboard is used in addition to a shooting script and a treatment. The sketches help the director and set and costume designers to visualize special effects, locations, and clothes. The storyboard may also help the cameraman, but the editor finds it useless because he cares only about footage. Animators usually employ a storyboard.

If you decide to use a script, don't look on it as a finished piece of work or take it too seriously, no matter how elaborately you have typed it. Be cavalier; at best it is merely a draft. Avoid using words abstractly. Some scripts are like poems but don't evoke pictures. Remember that the camera is going to have to record physical realities

105

—objects, places, actions. In fact, the action may determine the picture, so if you tell in the script what is happening, you may have a sense of what the movie will look like. If the heart of the film is clear to you, the details will work themselves out during the shooting. Don't be rigid about following the script. Use it to hold firm your point of view so that your first germ of an idea is still there in the finished film, but allow room for details that come to you spontaneously as you go along and that seem to enhance the central theme.

When you begin to formulate a film idea, try to tell someone about it as if you had already watched it on screen. Good storytellers can sometimes bring a movie they've seen to life so successfully that the listener feels no need to see it for himself. If you can describe your movie that way, your vision stands a good chance of being realized on film.

A treatment that seems self-explanatory to you may not communicate your ideas to someone else. When I read Karen's treatment for *The Breakfast,* I visualized an elegant room with French doors, beyond which were rain and mist; a young couple sat in front of the doors drinking coffee from fine china cups. The scene that was ultimately filmed from that script took place in a one-room tenement with a bathtub in the kitchen area; a bamboo blind hung over the cracked window so you couldn't see outdoors; the couple drank their coffee from chipped mugs. If the script suggests specific pictures to the person or people directing the filming, it is adequate, even if no one else can interpret it precisely.

This treatment was used by Alfonso in making The End. *If you compare it to the description of the film (pp. 38-41), you will notice that while the film underwent superficial changes, the basic vision remained consistent. There are personal notations, such as the ones for Scene Three which repeat "blur," with arrows pointing in various directions, to indicate swish pans. Notice how evocative of picture and action this script is.*

106

"THE TRUE DREAM"

by Alfonso Sanchez Jr.

Scene #1   Shot of president Johnson with two
           joints in his pocket, A hand taking one
           of them.

Scene #2   The guy walking to the room and lighting
           up and smoking it. Close ups of the guy looking
           high and going in to a dream

Scene #3   Blur → Blur ← Blur ↓ Blur ↑ Stop

Scene #4 → Close up of the guy on stage dancing open to
           wide angle, the guy dancing looking happy, the
           guy is dress with a black suit and top hat & cane

Scene #5   Shot at the andiance (empty seats)

Scene #6   Girls coming from back stage dancing with the guy
           all styes of dancing - boogaloo - shake - twist-
           karate boogaloo.

Scene #7   The guy sitting down in the park alone with
           nobody around him. The guy is reading a News-
           paper. Shots wide angle about 400 ft away from
           him, Deference reactions in his face, while looking
           at the pictures in the paper. He opens to the middle
           page and sees "pot is Legal" he jumps up looking
           happy trows the newspaper away. Blur → Blur ←

Scene #8   Close up of a police man in a corner swinging his
           club, the police man calls the guy fera a light
           the guy give him a light, the cop has a joint in his
           mouth while the guy is smoking one to ——→ Blur
           Blur ←

                              Look in the back ——————→

Scene #9   the guy running stopping at a building and then
           a man in black passing him. The guy sees him
           and he starts running away at slow motion
Scene #10 The guy stops at another building and then
           another man in white show up the guy looks
           at him and reaction in his face and starts

           running
Scene #11 the guy meeting the man in black, the
           man in black give him a bible. The man in
           black disappear. the guy keeps on going with
           the bible.
Scene #12 the guy meeting the man in white now
           the man in white takes away the bible
           and gives him a LSD tablet and a couple
           a bags. the man in white disappears
Scene #13 The guy keeps on walking with the bible
           and the tablet + bags
Scene #14 Man in black + white with american flags and
           shaking hands and disappearing.
Scene #15 The guy runs after he sees them disappearing.
           he's running slow motion.
Scene #16 The guy getting to his apartment knocking
           on the door
Scene #17 Inside the apartment the guy waking
           up and going to the door, he picks thru the
           pickhole and sees himself. He gets scared and
           runs to his bathroom.

Scene #18 the guy waking up walking to the door
            looking thru the pickhole

Scene #19 Shot of "what happening in this world."
            Shots of the war in Vietnam pictures (stills)
            Johnsons, soldiers, the guy, Man in white,
            man in black, with american flags

Scene #20 blur ⟶ blur ⟵ blur ↑ blur ↓

Scene #21 Shot of the guys hand taking the last
            joint ⟶ blur   THE END
                            Cool iT

                    by Alfonso Sanchez jr.

            Cast: Robert Bonilla   man in black
        Man in white Gilbert Serrano
        the dreamer - Benny Hernandez
                        ⎫ Neomi Hernandez
            the   ⎬ - Toni Rivera
          dancing   ⎭ Judy torres
            girl   Kona Shuman
        the cop - Jaime Barrios

WHEN YOUR IDEA FOR THE FILM HAS MATERIALIZED AND YOU ARE eager to start filming, ask yourself a few questions. Exactly where are you going to film? What problems might arise on location? If a scene is to be shot indoors, do you have adequate electrical outlets and extension cords for photoflood lights? If you are shooting in a public street, is a permit required by the traffic department? For outdoor scenes what time of day will be best in terms of natural light or background action? Alfonso answered this last question by filming a scene at 6 A.M. in an ordinarily busy street because he wanted to show it empty.

If you are filming in someone's home, be sure you are welcome. If your host is hovering about, worrying over his furniture, you will find it hard to concentrate. Hollywood films have enormous budgets, which provide for construction of towns, cities, and landscapes inside gigantic studios. This enables commercial filmmakers to control lighting, traffic, background action, and other aspects of production. The young filmmaker finds it more practical to use real locations, and he tends to feel that authenticity is gained this way.

Certain factors will be beyond your control. In *Look at Me* Cathy wanted to show a little boy climbing a snow-covered hill. She formulated the idea in September and for weeks thereafter kept calling the weather bureau, hoping for a forecast of snow. Her actor was ever on the alert, ready to dash to the hill when the first flakes appeared. Finally, one Saturday morning, it did snow, and Cathy did shoot her picture.

Andy, who made *That Rotten Teabag,* later used a seaside location during the summer for *Cecile Comes to Southampton.* The film is in a free-form documentary style and shows an old fisherman and

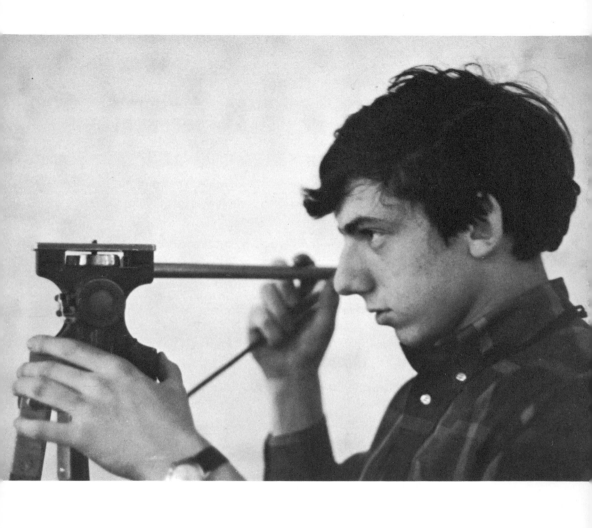

his family. This kind of film has to be created entirely in the editing. Six months after Andy got his original footage he was still dissatisfied. It was now winter in Southampton. What he did was unexpected and imaginative. He had teen-age actors reenact the life of the real family, in the same setting but at a different season. He made his comment by juxtaposing pictures of trees in full leaf with pictures of trees covered with snow; where the real family is on the lawn, the actors appear in a snowbank. Andy did not wait for the seasons to change. He adapted in a striking manner to the situation that confronted him.

Problems will always arise. Don't be discouraged or defeated. There will be a constant clash between realities and your imagined ideal. How you get around and overcome these obstacles depends on your ingenuity. Hollywood minimizes problems of weather and setting by using studios. When you're spending $20,000 a day, you don't want to stand around waiting for the sun to come out.

You will learn from experience to foresee and avoid certain potential difficulties. The first time Ivan photographed actors engaged in a street chase it never occurred to him to notify the local police precinct of what he was going to do. He—and the rest of us at FILM CLUB— came to see the wisdom of such notification. We already knew, because we had asked, that policemen could not get permission to appear in our films. Ivan settled for actors as plainclothesmen and bought toy pistols for them. On a busy street he began filming in his accustomed cinéma vérité style, holding the camera in his hand. The two actor-detectives jumped from an automobile and drew their toy pistols on actors portraying young thugs. By chance a patrol car rounded the corner at that moment. They saw the men with guns, but they did not see Ivan's camera. The real-life police drew their real guns on the actors. Someone cried out, "They're making a movie! Don't shoot!" Ivan, a true filmmaker, kept right on filming and later used the shot of the actual policemen running into the scene. The police told Ivan that if in future he planned to film a dramatization of street violence, he should notify the local precinct in advance so an officer could be on hand to explain to other policemen and to passersby what was happening. Commercial filmmakers work very closely with the police department in connection with filming on location. Our own experience has been that the police are very cooperative if we get permission through the desk sergeant, who notifies the cop on the beat. You can rent a realistic policeman's uniform for an actor, but you should still get clearance from your local desk sergeant before the actor appears outside.

Make a list of props before you arrive on the scene ready to shoot. Remember the trouble Jesus had with the wine bottle in *An Unpleasant Evening?* Get everything together and keep an eye on details. This applies not only to props but to actors. If they are filmed on several days in what will be one scene in the final movie, they should wear the same clothes and hair styles each time.

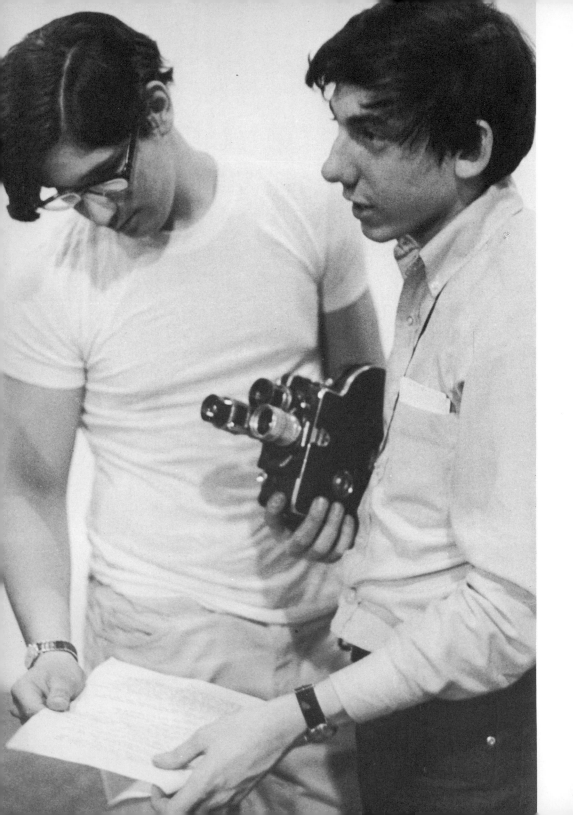

DURING A SEMINAR FOR TEEN-AGERS WHICH I GAVE AT NEW YORK'S
Metropolitan Museum of Art, the Peterson brothers, Gregory and
Maurice, who had made five films by the age of sixteen, showed some
of them. Maurice addressed the audience first with a few impromptu
remarks about his experiences:

"I guess the most difficult thing [is] to get people to show up. So
my advice if any of you want to start doing movies is don't ever work
with more than three people, tops, unless you're working in school
where they have to be in school on time every day, or like in a camp
or something. Do not rely on more than three people because it just
won't work. And also it would be nice if you're working with a girl
[to] make sure her hair is short because girls have this habit of cutting their hair in the middle of this picture where you're doing it
with long hair. And just keep it so that you know who's in control
and know what you're doing. Have everything written out before you
start, unless it's going to be a chancy thing where you just go out
and film things, you know, like film buildings or something. If you're
having a script, have everything written out. Know exactly what
you're doing before you do it."

Acting seems to come naturally to young people who are asked
to appear in their friends' films. This is partly because teen movies
call for a lot of action, and being constantly in motion relieves the
actors of self-consciousness. A film is shot in short takes, and the
sustained performances required by the theatre are unnecessary.
There are seldom lines to memorize, and there is no audience to be
nervous about. Casting young people is not usually troublesome because the filmmaker instinctively chooses friends whose own per-

115

sonalities are similar to the characters they are to play. If a script calls for an older person, the director may feel awkward about telling him what to do, but I have seen a young director work authoritatively with an actor three times his age. The worst actors are animals. They never seem to do what the director wants while the camera is turning. Unless you plan to shoot the entire film in one day, as John Earl did, keep your cast as small as possible. Perhaps a few more people than the three Maurice suggested are manageable.

A lot of makeup looks phony in close-ups. Boys usually don't wear any. Girls can do their own but should be told to go lightly. The camera is so truthful that you can't make a youngster look old by applying makeup; it is best to get a person who looks the appropriate age. I don't mean to say that you should never use makeup. In *Memory of John Earl* John's face was supposed to be cut and bloody, an effect he achieved by mixing instant-coffee powder and ketchup and applying this mixture as makeup. In fantasies you may need makeup to create offbeat faces. Or you may want to show someone who in real life wears heavy makeup, perhaps a clown or an older woman who tries to paint on a younger face.

If you work with an actor who has some stage experience and considers himself competent, you will probably have to tone down his performance. On film, gestures and facial expressions must be underplayed in order to be convincing when they are magnified on screen. Professional movie actors often watch the dailies, but with amateurs it is better if they do not see themselves on film until the shooting is complete; once they become self-critical, they lose some of their spontaneity.

In choosing a friend to play a part in your film, keep in mind two requirements: that he and the character have traits in common and that the character never does anything that would be completely foreign to your friend. Ask if he would like to be in your movie. It

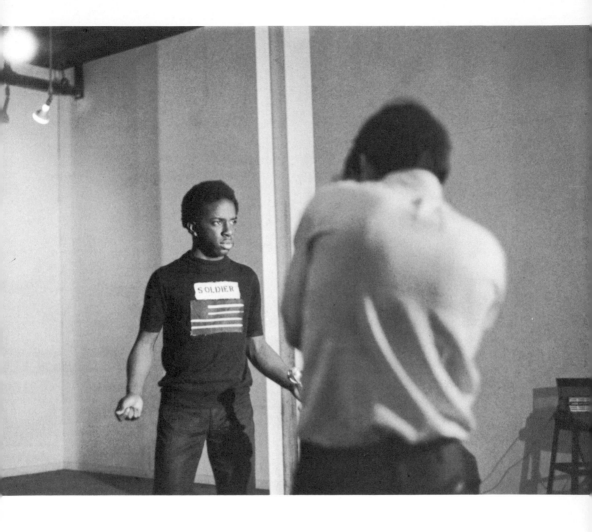

is likely that after short hesitation he will say yes. He has been presented with the opportunity to behold the mystery of himself. Few of us can resist this temptation, so ask with self-assurance. Then approach the other people you need, telling them who has already accepted.

Nobody can really anticipate the amount of time actors will have to spend just waiting. They wait for the camera to be ready, for the lens to be focused for each take, for the sun to come out from behind clouds, for misplaced props to be located. Waiting drives amateur actors crazy. They become petulant and irritable. They can't understand why everything takes so long. You have to adjust to this and learn to deal with them. Explain your technical problems to them and enlist their sympathies. Have food handy, especially in the morning, since you will often go past lunchtime. Don't encourage actors to read or play games like checkers because just as they become absorbed, you will need them.

You will be busy every second. Remain calm. The director is in a vulnerable position when he is imposing on his friends to donate their services. The reward of seeing themselves in a finished movie is months away, and they are only conscious of the here and now. Since actors may try to take advantage of you, you must be careful to maintain your authority. Pamper, charm, or coerce according to which you do most successfully. Keep in mind what your priorities are: getting the film finished takes precedence over being popular with your cast. Not that your cast need be a collective enemy. Actors can be exhilarated after a day of strenuous shooting if the director knew what he was doing, they enjoyed their parts, and they believed in the film.

The director has many responsibilities in addition to keeping his cast in line. He may be his own cameraman, and in any event he must direct the cameraman. If you are the cameraman, your mind and

119

energies are divided. You have to know what is going on in front of as well as inside the camera. You need to keep a delicate balance. If you are all cameraman, you may end up with well-taken pictures of meaningless subject matter, and if you are all director, you may elicit the world's greatest performances only to find that the film comes back from the laboratory unviewable. A classic example is the cameraman-director who filmed a whole scene with no film in the camera.

Technically, the watchword is caution; its corollary is double-check. Every location has built-in pitfalls. To beat them is half the fun. It also helps to be flexible enough to turn accidents to your own advantage. When Nancy was shooting, it began to snow and she made an effort to keep flakes off the lens by holding an umbrella over the camera. It didn't work and most of the footage was very fuzzy. At first she was unhappy, but then she came to like the soft, out-of-focus quality. Other filmmakers might have reshot the scene without falling snow. Rain on the lens will have the same effect as snowflakes. Direct sunlight on the lens creates refractions. Care should be taken to shield the lens. If you are filming almost directly into sunlight, you can hold the script over the lens to shade it, but it is better to position the camera so that it is not aiming toward the sun. If you are not the cameraman, you are responsible for making sure he is checking all these conditions.

The director and the cameraman must understand and respect each other's viewpoints. Achieving this rapport isn't easy and takes a certain amount of canny psychology. The only time the cameraman is justified in quarreling with the director is when he is asked for a shot the camera cannot get. If the director wants to show four people sitting around a room and the camera is backed against the wall and four people don't fit in the frame, then the cameraman has to say, "It won't work." The director must decide to shoot two people at a

121

time and edit together the separate shots, or to bring the four people closer together until they fit into the frame, or to ask the cameraman to go outside and shoot in through the window and so leave the original composition intact. The cameraman should not argue with the director's choice of alternatives.

Alfonso is one of the best teen-age directors I know. He engages his actors' interest, casts them because their own personalities reflect the characters' personalities, and listens to their ideas about camera angles, action, and plot. If he receives suggestions that are consistent with his own feelings, he incorporates them in his work. If not, he politely but firmly rejects them. Real authority is not rigid and unyielding but relaxed and in control. The authoritative director welcomes creative contributions from the people around him and also pays attention to his own impulses. As long as he has a sense of where it is all going, he can make room for details that were not preplanned.

If your film is to be shot over a period of several days, it is helpful to try out first an especially uncomplicated scene, perhaps one that requires a single actor. This gives you a chance to test your mettle. Based on the experience of the first day's shooting, you will form a sense of how to function. Remember that you do not need to shoot scenes in the same order that they appear in the script. Your shooting order is dictated by such considerations as completing all scenes in a given location before moving equipment to another location, and using the actors you have called together for a particular scene in other scenes where they appear together.

If time permits, get the film from your first day into and out of the laboratory immediately and run it on the projector before shooting more film. Studying the results, you will be able to determine picture quality, acting quality, and how well your imagination is translating onto film. Because the camera does not see the way your eyes see,

that early batch of film can provide one of the best learning experiences you will ever have. Do not be concerned about mistakes because so far the investment is minimal. You can make any mistake once, but if you make it more than once, you are being absentminded. Experienced teen-age filmmakers like to see each exposed reel as soon as possible. Professionals call these segments dailies, or rushes. As you view the dailies, you not only check on how you are doing, you often find plot ideas coming to you that you would have missed had you shot all in one day.

As you feel your way along, you will decide if you want the actors to walk through their parts before you film—in other words, if you want a rehearsal. Some teen-agers prefer this method because of the control it makes possible. They pay a price, however. Actors get fidgety and impatient and resent repetition, particularly if the action called for is tiring, like climbing stairs. They begin to feel like robots, and when the scene is finally shot, they may be stiff and wooden. For this reason other students prefer a cinéma vérité approach. They describe the scene to their actors and the cameraman, and film spontaneously without prior run-through. This, too, has drawbacks. The actors may do it wrong, move too fast or be too hesitant, walk out of the frame, or project inappropriate moods. Then the scene has to be reshot, and you have paid for film exposed on what was in fact a rehearsal.

In either case, you will probably need to shoot some scenes more than once. The beginning filmmaker likes to photograph everything at eye level from a medium distance, as if he is a spectator just looking on. Only the audience is a spectator. Your film will be made up of many pieces, and if you shoot a scene from varying levels, angles, and distances, you will provide yourself with greater possibilities later, when you are editing. As in *Mary Worth* (see page 129) a scene should be captured from several perspectives. Traditionally, the director first

125

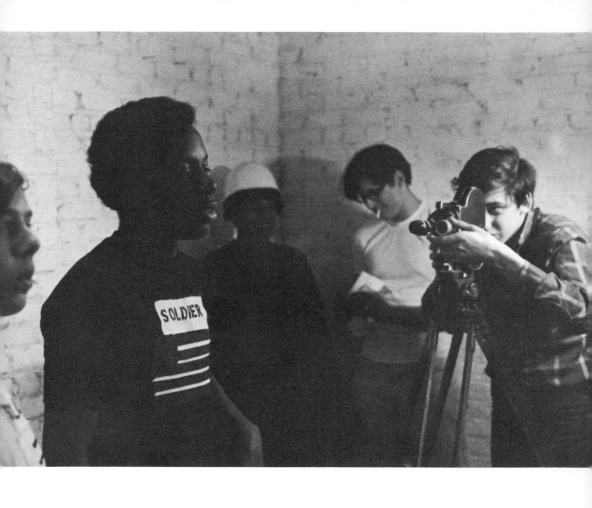

gets the master shot, which encompasses the whole scene in continuous action. Then the scene is replayed the same way and shot from a variety of angles in order to point up details.

In early films the camera took the position of the audience at a play. One of the first uses of an insert close-up to make a point is in D. W. Griffith's 1910 film, *The Last Deal*. Griffith showed a card game in progress and the camera stood back, taking in the whole scene (master shot). Suddenly onto the screen flashed a close-up of a player's cards. Griffith had been compelled to this innovation by his desire to show what cards the gambler held. The viewer was yanked out of his seat on the aisle and brought right up into the card game. Movies were transformed by such demonstrations that the camera could shift positions without disturbing the viewer.

FRAME A   CUT   FRAME B   CUT   FRAME C

FRAME A

Establishing shot sets the scene as it opens on the action with Seth standing at the door. The viewer is looking from behind Frank's desk.

Cut to:

FRAME B

Reverse angle. The viewer is now looking over Seth's shoulder. *Medium shot* (to show facial expressions). A few seconds have elapsed between frames because Seth now holds his hat in his hands (in a film this would be a jump cut).

Cut to:

FRAME C

Close-up of Seth. Viewer sees from Frank's point of view. We know that a split second has elapsed from Frame B to Frame C because Seth's hat is just slightly farther from his shoulder than before, as he begins to set it down (in film this would be a match cut).

129

c/o National Periodical Publications, Inc., 1969

FRAME A CUT FRAME B CUT FRAME C

FRAME A
Establishing shot (wide angle) reveals Batman, unconscious in a hospital room as Killer Killey is helped on with his shirt by the Mad Doctor.

Cut to:

FRAME B
Close-up of Mad Doctor. We know that time has elapsed because now the doctor's hands are free of Killer Killey's shirt. The doctor's speech is made more emphatic by close-up.

Cut to:

FRAME C
Close-up of Batman to reveal the doctor's work on his nose and hands.
Voice over picture. The scheming doctor's voice appears over the picture of Batman's helplessness. This juxtaposition heightens the dramatic situation.

130

Notice, in both comic strips, that emphasis is given to voice inflection by putting certain key words in larger letters. Some other comic strips that employ cinematic techniques are *Rex Morgan, M.D., Brenda Starr, Steve Canyon,* and *Dick Tracy*. Strips like *Peanuts* and *Nancy,* while they are delightful comics, do not use a movie-like construction.

Readers are hardly ever conscious of the complexity of comic-strip construction nor are moviegoers aware of most techniques of film. But the creators, both comic-strip artist and filmmaker, must understand their crafts and tools.

You can see, in these examples, how much of the information and experience comes through the picture, which adds so much to the dialogue.

Camera angles are not arbitrarily decided upon. Randy shot a scene in which an overbearing official confronts a meek little man. In real life the actors were the same height. With intelligent use of camera angles Randy conveyed forcefully the relationship between these two by creating a sense of physical as well as psychological disparity. He shot up at the official so that the man, as he looked down, seemed to be towering. Randy filmed the meek character from above so that he appeared to be looking up at his opponent and cowering. The mood is set, and when we see the two together, our impressions from the close-ups carry over.

In the days of silent movies, titles were inserted throughout the film to tell what actors were saying. Most of my students prefer to make their pictures self-explanatory and don't want written words to interrupt the flow. One boy did employ a letter as a device to further the plot; he shot so the viewer could read it over the actor's shoulder, but this is a weak way to impart information.

131

Breakfast
adapted from a poem by Jacques Prevert

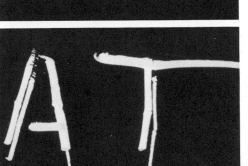

by Karen Wolf
with: Judith Kurtz
Bernard heri
and: Michael Bady
cameraman

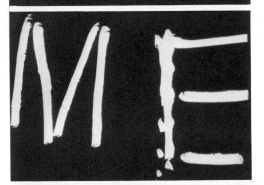

CECILE
COMES
TO
SOUTHAMPTON

STUDENTS OCCASIONALLY LIKE TO SHOOT SCREEN CREDITS FIRST OF all. There are student films that are half credits and are so elaborate that they hold your interest. The simplest and most popular way to do screen credits is to take a piece of blank typing paper and write the credits on it with a black felt-tipped marker, stick it on a wall with masking tape, and film it. Some directors like to integrate the credits into the texture of the film. Jesus spray-painted his on the park wall and panned over them. Cathy scratched the words "Look at Me" on film. She wrote "look" thirty-two times and the other two words twenty-four times. On screen the words flashed white and bouncy. She did it this way because she was rushing to meet the deadline of a film festival and did not have time to shoot credits, but it turned out nicely.

Andy and Randy in one picture they did together took plastic letters from a lettering kit and animated them. They scrambled the letters, then arranged them for a credit, then scrambled them and put them in new order for the next. On screen the letters appeared to be scrambling and unscrambling of their own accord. Karen sketched her film title on a scrap of spiral notebook paper that turned out to be the wrong shape to fit the viewfinder frame. She had been admiring another girl's paisley print dress so she borrowed it, put it on the floor, dropped the scrap of paper on top of it, and filmed it. Initially Karen didn't realize that with both 8mm and 16mm film, the frame size has a 3:4 ratio. Compose your credits with this ratio in mind unless you plan to pan as Jesus did. The question often comes up of how long the credits should run on screen. Read the words slowly through the viewfinder as you are filming. When you finish reading the words, you have the proper length.

133

Shooting the picture provides raw material for a finished film. While the movie is being shot, the action stops and starts and the whole experience usually seems disjointed. All the pieces, the master shots, inserts, and facial close-ups should come together during the editing phase into a smoothly flowing entity.

HERE'S AN EXPERIMENT FOR YOU, THE EDITOR-TO-BE, TO BRING HOME the realization that film is, like a mosaic, composed of many tiny pieces and that when they are properly put together, the viewer has a sense of flow and is not conscious of cuts. Check out a movie on television, setting a kitchen timer for sixty seconds and counting the number of cuts that occur. In that minute, 1,440 frames, or 36 feet of film, go by. There may be only four cuts or there may be fifteen to twenty. Concentrate not on continuity but on these small segments that make up the whole. Imagine how many little bits of film are spliced together for an hour-and-a-half feature film. You may hereafter find yourself seeing movies in terms of cuts and for a while losing the overall perspective; eventually you will take cuts into account without being distracted by them.

When all the footage is assembled, it seems terribly long and needs a lot of work. You have to disassociate yourself from the cameraman, even if he was you, and become an editor. You take off one hat and don another. The first time you try the editor's hat you will probably feel a conflict because you will remember how hard it was to get all that film and be proud of every beautifully photographed shot. In one sense, it would be easier to edit film you had never seen before because you must ruthlessly select those pieces that will make the best possible construction and discard all others.

At this point you may discover that the vitality your movie seemed to have when you were cameraman-director has disappeared. Everything on screen will seem to take much longer than it did in real life; this is a fact of film experience. Screen time is very different from clock time. Luis coped with this in *The Flop*. There was a scene where his main actor was eating breakfast alone in the kitchen. Luis shot it in a logical manner: (1) boy enters the room, (2) goes to the refrigerator, (3) removes milk carton, (4) gets cereal from cupboard, (5) sits at table, pours cereal, adds milk and sugar, stirs it, (6) eats in a hurry, (7) gets up from table, (8) puts bowl in sink, (9) returns cereal to shelf and (10) milk to refrigerator. When Luis saw this assemblage, he groaned and said, "It's very boring." How could he convey the action without its seeming interminable?

Of all the fascinating experiences editing affords, manipulating time is the most intriguing. Luis had planned his film so that a scene followed that breakfast in which the boy's friend came to his apartment to meet him and they then left the building together. The same problem arose here: (a) friend walks down street, (b) climbs front steps, (c) opens door, (d) climbs interior stairs, (e) knocks on apartment door. It seemed awfully dull. Luis manipulated time and pictures in editing to achieve excellent pacing and his film came alive. This is how he intercut: (3) boy removes milk carton from refrigerator, (a) friend walks down street, (6) boy eats cereal, (d) friend climbs interior stairs, (10) boy returns milk to refrigerator, (e) friend knocks on apartment door. Luis was able to condense screen time without suggesting that the action was frantic. The viewer fills in the missing actions during this scene; they are suggested rather than detailed.

The only filmmaker I know of who has used clock time as screen time is Andy Warhol. He has run the camera nonstop on his actors and simply put the film on the projector the way it came from the camera without making a single deletion. But even he, in his more recent films, stops and starts the camera in order to condense screen action. Editing is the crux of most successful filmmaking, and Mr. Warhol is a rare exception in being able to get around this.

Occasionally the filmmaker may need to extend time so that it is longer on screen then it was in real life. Elliott wanted to convey a

138

mood of reluctance as two fellows in his film approached the desk of a frightening judge. On screen he made their walk to the desk twice as long as the length of the room they were in. The first shot was taken from behind the desk, over the judge's shoulder. The second shot was from a reverse angle, and the camera was shifted 180 degrees to a position in the door opposite the desk. First we watch from the desk as the boys walk the length of the room. Then there is a cut back to the door and we watch from there as they walk the same distance. It sounds as if the viewer would think the boys jumped back to their starting point for the second shot, but the actual effect is of their walking twice the real distance.

The film editor wants to weed out the superfluous so that the telling moments are captured. As he huddles over the film viewer, he should constantly "Cut on the action." That means cut to the frame where the action begins and discard the preceding few frames, hold the action on screen until it is completed, and cut immediately. If you are showing a man striking out with his fist at another man's jaw, pick up the fist just as it begins to move forward, and the instant it contacts the jaw cut away to a reaction shot of the face being hit. Or show the fist coming at the camera and then cut to a reaction shot at a different angle. Be sure the action is thoroughly completed. If a man is sitting down in a chair and the scene is cut before he quite touches it, it is disconcerting to say the least. "Action" does not necessarily imply large gestures. In *That Rotten Teabag* it was action when the tea bag was shifted from cup to saucer. As with a comic strip, the viewer automatically makes assumptions that fill in missing actions if significant ones are portrayed.

Continuity of shots is often desirable so that a scene flows smoothly from one cut to another. This is achieved through match cuts. In *The Revenge,* which was a group effort, there was an establishing shot of a homesteader waving his right hand to visitors. Later on the di-

139

rector wanted a medium shot of the same scene and the actor waved his left hand. The mistake was discovered only in editing. What we saw was the homesteader waving his right hand followed by a closer view of his left hand in the air. It looked ridiculous. How to salvage the scene? Sometimes you can't; even professionals have unsolvable problems of this sort. After carefully scanning the footage, the editor discovered that the homesteader lowered his right arm after waving the first time. In the medium shot there was an instant where both arms hung down before the left one went up. As the scene finally appeared, the homesteader waves his right hand, drops his arm, and then waves his left hand.

Some filmmakers find jump cuts liberating and delight in their use, while others find them jarring and abhor them. A jump cut implies that a relevant piece of action is missing. (See *Mary Worth,* page 129, cut between frames A and B.) In *The End* Alfonso uses a jump cut in the final sequence where Benny awakes from his marijuana reverie, hears a knock at the door, and gets out of bed to answer it. Alfonso cuts from a shot of Benny quickly sitting up in bed to a shot of Benny walking toward the door. This says, Benny is nervous and jumpy. Showing Benny literally getting out of bed would have made him seem too relaxed. There are situations where a jump cut is inappropriate. Murray originally jump cut from his grandmother eating to her washing dishes. On screen she seemed to be dashing from place to place, and he wanted her actions to be methodical. By slowing down the pace through intercutting portraits of her family which hung on the wall, he said quite a few things; one was that the people in the photographs dominated his grandmother's thoughts as she went about her tasks.

It is crucial to develop editing procedures that are comfortable for you and to stick to them. After you have seen the film projected several times, you must "break down the rushes." This is always scary

for the beginner. You cut apart with scissors each roll of film so that individual shots are separated. Shots that you think belong in the film should be hung in the film bin. Outtakes, or pieces that you don't expect to use, should be rolled up and fastened with a bit of masking tape on which you have written a brief description of that shot. Don't throw away outtakes. Store them in a box or can so that if you change your mind later you can quickly retrieve them. Beginners often throw outtakes onto the floor and then into a wastebasket. Weeks later they discover that some of that footage is just what they need and it's too late.

A professional film bin is a metal bin lined with a flannel bag, above which is a rack studded with pins or hooks. Individual shots are hung up by their sprocket holes and their tails fall into the flannel bag; long pieces of film can safely nestle there. The film bin is on wheels so it can be moved about. You can improvise with an empty chemical or soap-powder barrel; your school janitor may have one he will part with. There is a simpler method which works in a temporary editing setup. Take a large shopping bag and tape it a few inches from the floor on the wall of your bedroom (or wherever you edit). Fasten the film strips you are considering onto the wall with masking tape so that the ends fall into the bag. Label each shot on the tape. If you have a lot of film, you may use three bags—one for the beginning, one for the middle, and one for the end of your movie. Keep all film away from dampness and heat.

When handling film strips, get in the habit of being conscious of the head (beginning of shot) and the tail (end of shot). Always hang shots with the head up. You can locate it by looking at a frame: the heads of the actors should be on top, as should the sky. Also learn to hang film with the emulsion side facing out. These habits will make the job of assembling pictures much easier because you can pull a piece of film from the bin or wall and set it into the splicer with

142

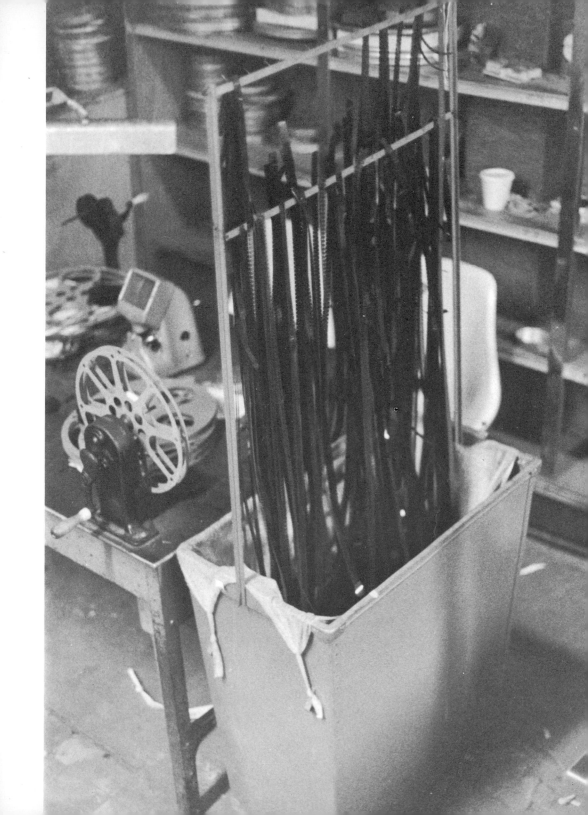

complete confidence that the scene is not upside down or reversed. If you have to spend half an hour looking for a shot you misplaced or did not label properly or figuring out which way the piece goes in the splicer, the creative process will be hampered. You really have to be organized to save your energy for creative decisions.

The splicer is the editing tool with which individual shots are fastened together in the desired sequence. I recommend use of a wet splicer. It is designed to cement pieces of film together. Emulsion is scraped from the edge of the head with a single-edged razor or emery board, and the head is wet with cement and joined to the tail of the previous shot. The tail is not scraped, but for a firmer splice it can be wet with cement. The other splicing tool sold in photo stores is a tape or butt splicer. It butts the head of one shot with the tail of the previous one and fastens them with clear mylar sprocketed tape. Tape splices break. They disfigure four frames (two on either side of the splice) instead of only two, as with wet splices. Many laboratories refuse to make prints if tape splices have been used because they are difficult to work with. That is why I prefer wet splicers. A well-made cement splice is stronger than the film itself. There is no excuse for a cement splice breaking in the projector. If it does, the probable cause is that the cement was too old, the emulsion was not completely removed from the head, or the cement was not allowed to dry thoroughly before the film was removed from the splicer (fifteen seconds are necessary).

Film cement has volatile ingredients, which fuse acetate surfaces. If a bottle of cement is left open, it loses its adhering qualities and should be thrown away. Keep the bottle capped between splices. This cement eats through varnished surfaces and asphalt, so an enamel- or Formica-topped kitchen table is useful for editing.

The only other indispensable tools for the editor are a film viewer and a pair of rewinds. For 8mm films these are usually combined in

a single piece of equipment. For 16mm they are usually separate. The film viewer resembles a large slide viewer. It is electrical and uses a light bulb just as a slide viewer does. As the film passes through the viewer, the image is magnified on its screen. A shutter flicks closed and open quickly between each frame, providing an instant of blackness to give the impression of motion. (See persistence of vision, page 79.) Rewinds permit the editor to wind film through the viewer at his own tempo instead of at the 24FPS of a projector. He can stop the film and run it backward and forward to determine exactly where to make his cut. Rewinds are attached to the table or to the viewer. The full reel of film slides onto a spindle on the lefthand rewind, film head up; then the film passes through the viewer to a reel on the righthand rewind which takes it up. Attached to the spindle of each rewind is a handle which the editor turns manually.

Brief instructions for the beginning film editor:

1. Take a blank piece of film two or three feet long and splice the head of the first shot to it. This is head leader. Later splice a blank piece of film to the tail of the last shot of the movie as tail leader.
2. As each splice is made, wind it up on the righthand rewind. Get accustomed to movement from left to right.
3. Always take care to leave extra frames at each splice. Until the fine cut, let shots be too long. You lose at least two frames with each splice and they cannot be put back.
4. Sometimes a single frame at the beginning or end of a shot is overexposed to whiteness when the camera stops and the shutter remains open. These frames should be weeded out.
5. Don't be in a hurry to make a fine cut. Wait until the entire rough cut is assembled before completing any one scene.

6. The projector regulates the actual pacing of the movie. Don't be deceived by the length of a scene in the viewer. Keep returning to the projector to get an accurate sense of timing and to study your assemblage.

7. Pieces removed at this stage are called trims. If they are more than twenty-four frames, they, too, should be marked and stored, as were outtakes.

8. Moving toward a fine cut, you may think about removing only three or four frames at a time. This is not splitting hairs. Three or four extra frames on several scenes may add up to seconds of total running time, and this subtle excess is guaranteed to rob your movie of vitality. Mark unwanted frames with a grease pencil. You'll see the grease marks when the film is run through the projector and get a firmer impression of whether or not the frames are needed. Three frames too few can be as disastrous as three too many.

Film should be treated with great care throughout all this viewing, reviewing, splicing, and resplicing. With rough handling the emulsion receives scratches from loose dust particles. Dust scratches and dirt become painfully apparent when the film is projected, and they are magnified, so work in a clean area. Most 8mm filmmakers do all their editing on original reversal, and neatness and cleanliness are especially important when handling original film. A few teen-agers working with 16mm may be fortunate enough to have a work print to edit; when a fine cut is achieved, they cut the original, which will never have gone through the projector or viewer, to match frame-by-frame the work print. Invariably film will pick up fingerprints and dirt as it is handled. When this happens, take a soft cloth saturated with movie-film cleaner, run the film from one rewind to the other, and pass it through the saturated cloth in your hand rather than

through the viewer. This will remove skin oils and loose dirt. Scratches are permanent.

Generally, editors find a way, with the film they have, to do what they want. Sometimes, however, they may have to reshoot. Nancy discovered in her rough cut that she had taken no close-ups and felt she needed them to reveal her heroine. The most inventive editing couldn't solve her problem. At first she despaired because her movie was set in the snow and the snow had melted. Finally she realized that she could take such tight shots that the background scenery would not show. She ran the film, took careful note of the actress's hair style and clothes and of what hand she held her school books in and then reshot the needed close-ups to match existing footage.

It's smart to shoot more film than you think you need. Don't just take the peak of the action and don't just cover a scene from one angle at one distance. Be prepared later to throw out the extraneous material. When you become that hunched-over figure at the viewer, you will be grateful to the cameraman-director you were earlier for allowing plenty of leeway. It would be nice if you could visualize when you are filming exactly what you will and won't need later on, but you can't. You never really know what a scene will look like on film until you see it projected. I have visited locations and people after seeing them in a movie, and in real life they looked quite unfamiliar. The film version gave me the impression of greater space and size. Because images are magnified on screen, your sense of scale is thrown off. Movies seem so real but they aren't. A smile may be six feet wide, and if later you are met by that same smile in real life, it is apt to seem less impressive. As editor, you adjust your original vision to what you have on film.

The fine cut is the final version of a movie. As you approach it, leave in any shot you doubt until you become absolutely certain about what should be done with it. Such certainty may come only after repeated viewings of the film as a whole. You do not have a fine cut until your ambivalence about any given scene has become either a confirmed decision to take it out or an assurance that it belongs. You should be satisfied with the length and selection of each individual piece in the fine cut, unless you relate to your films as D. W. Griffith did to his and never feel content. He needed constantly to experiment with new juxtapositions; there was no sound on his early films, so this was possible. If you have an optical sound track, revision will affect it adversely. Some filmmakers feel that as beauty includes flaws, so their films are richer for the imperfections. You will probably discover that you can create a fine cut which pleases you.

WHEN RANDY WAS BEGINNING HIS FIRST 16MM MOVIE, HE DECIDED to play a record of the sound track of his favorite movie as mood music while filming. On the opening day of shooting, as he organized actors, lights, props, and camera, barely fifteen minutes had elapsed before he barked, "Turn that damned thing off!" He had quickly realized that music had nothing to do with the tasks at hand. It was not until after he had assembled the picture that he began again to think in musical terms. The beginner, in particular, ought to concentrate on a movie's visual aspects until he has them under control. When you work with a silent camera, as most teen-agers do, the nature of the sound track which will be added later often seems remote and undefined—except where a haunting melody or song sparked the film idea. The synchronous camera records images and sounds simultaneously: single-system synchronous cameras record sound in the camera on the film's magnetic stripe; double-system models synchronize the film with quarter-inch tape on an attached synchronous recorder. Synchronous models are too complicated to describe here.

A sound track brings a new dimension to a film. Many students spend as much time in working out their sound tracks as in cutting their pictures because they feel the films will be richer for the addition. There are several ways to provide sound. The simplest is to play a record during a screening. Or you can put sound on tape to be played with the film: records of music or of dramatic readings, friends playing an original composition, noises of traffic, crowds, birdsongs, and so forth. Judy went into a subway with a battery-operated portable tape recorder to capture the racket in a tunnel for a subway scene she had filmed earlier with a silent camera.

Records of sound effects are readily available in record shops and in some libraries. A typical sound-effects record has everything from noises of an airport control tower to those of the lion house at a zoo. In *The Tell-Tale Heart,* Bill used a medical recording of a human heartbeat. Electronic sounds can be improvised with a guitar amplifier by experimenting with the reverb. Susan got some highly original sounds for *Life Is Just a Bowl of Cherries* by recording through a guitar amplifier and slapping the side of it occasionally—working in the same spirit as when she kicked the table to make the vegetables jiggle.

Narration can contribute to a film. It should not duplicate what the picture makes obvious. A few words go a long way, so keep it brief. José employed descriptive passages spoken by a narrator to convey plot in *Flash.* Don't overlook the fact that some passages of film can be made more forceful by the absence of sound. A silent moment will underscore what is happening on screen.

A mix is always used in professional films. From two to twelve separate tracks are combined by rerecording them simultaneously onto a single track. An inexpensive mixer can be bought at local electronic shops and will allow you to feed two or more tracks into one tape recording and to overlap, fade-in, and fade-out sounds. You can record narration over music or combine other single tracks. Since all tracks to be recorded must run simultaneously during mixing, you will need at the very least two tape recorders or a live mike and a tape recorder or two live mikes. The quarter-inch tape with the combined tracks on it can be played on a tape recorder beside the projector or transferred to a 16mm optical track or to a magnetic stripe on film.

When putting sounds on tape for a movie, place the projector and tape recorder in different rooms so the projector's noise won't be picked up on tape; if possible, project through a glass door. As the film runs, you attempt to coordinate the sounds you are putting on tape with the pictures on screen. A stop watch can help you. Record at seven and a half inches per second (or the fastest speed on your

tape recorder) and use tape that has already been recorded on and completely erased; having been prestretched by use, such tape will stay in better synchronization. Quarter-inch tape can be spliced with a tape splicer and magnetic sound splicing tape. Be sure records are scratch- and dust-free so that sound quality is preserved. When you play your taped sound track during screenings, try to use the same tape recorder and projector used for the original synchronization. Different machines run at slightly different speeds, and the timing will be thrown off by changing your equipment.

In order to lock sound to picture in perfect synchronization, the sound must be attached to the acetate. This is done in one of two ways: (1) If a narrow magnetic sound stripe is put on either 8mm or 16mm film, you then record sound into the projector using a mike, tape recorder, or turntable. The magnetic stripe is located on the edge opposite the sprocket holes of single-perforated film (sprocket holes on one edge only). When film with a stripe is played on a projector equipped for it, synchronization is good but not necessarily perfect. (2) The ultimate in 16mm sound on film is the optical track. Sound is transferred to 16mm magnetic sprocketed tape from the film's recorded magnetic stripe. Or it is transferred from recorded quarter-inch tape (the quarter-inch tape must have been recorded on one track and one side only). The sound is now on the 16mm magnetic sprocketed tape. The next step is to transfer sound from the magnetic tape to film and so to make an optical track. This optical track is combined with the picture on one piece of single-sprocketed film; the sound is along the edge opposite the sprocket holes. The combination of optical track with picture is called a composite print. Optical sound can actually be seen if you hold the film up to the light. In the projector, as the composite unrolls, the sounds on film pass through a beam of light from the exciter lamp and are made audible by the amplifier built into the projector. Some projectors have built-in speakers, too.

156

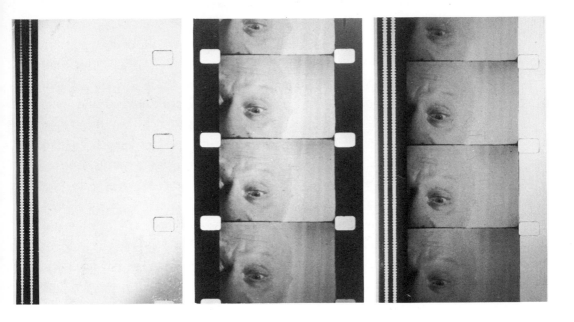

optical track   *original reversal*   *composite print*

Where speakers are on connecting cables, they should be placed under the screen.

The most important tools of the professional sound editor are the Movieola and the synchronizer, which enable him to align the 16mm magnetic sound track perfectly with the picture and to interlock them. The Movieola plays the 16mm magnetic sprocketed sound tape through a small speaker and the work print (pictures) through a small viewer simultaneously. It is motor-driven and runs both film and tape at 24FPS. The synchronizer, which has a small speaker attached to it, is manually operated and is placed beside a tape splicer. They sit between a pair of rewinds. The work print (picture) reel and the 16mm magnetic sprocketed tape (sound) reel are slipped together onto the lefthand rewind's spindle. The tape is spliced to fit sound to image, and tape and film are then aligned in the synchronizer. They are wound onto the take-up reels on the righthand rewind. The process of making an optical sound track, although fascinating, is expensive and requires an expert's help.

Even without synchronous sound equipment you can include dialogue as well as sound effects. The actors say their lines during filming and are not recorded. Later they dub their lines into a microphone while watching the movie and matching their words to the lip movements on screen. This is called lip sync. It can also be accomplished with a magnetic stripe by recording actors' lines on tape during filming and using a synchronizer later to align sound and picture for a composite optical print. From movies about big-time movies in Hollywood you are probably familiar with the sight of a man who stands with a small slate on which are written the scene and take numbers. At the beginning of each take he slams down a bar of wood hinged to the top of the slate and calls out loudly the numbers recorded there. Later the editor finds the moment on the sound tape where the wood strikes, and aligns it with the picture of the wood clicking

158

shut. You won't be using synchronous sound equipment, but you may want to use a modified slate if you plan to record lines on tape on location. You can write the scene and take numbers in a spiral notebook and hold up the page to the camera at the beginning of each take, reading the numbers aloud. When you get to the synchronizer, you will attempt to match lip movements with words. Don't expect perfection with this method, since you did not have a synchronous camera and tape recorder.

It is a great thrill to hear your screen characters talk, but sync sound and even lip sync are too much for most beginners to undertake. They are expensive and elaborate and distract you from learning about visual expressiveness. With lip sync, amateur actors often become wooden, the cameraman's attention is divided, and the editor gets hopelessly lost. Simple dubbing in of a few lines of dialogue, rather than of an entire script, is tedious for a beginner, but occasionally essential. John did this very effectively in *Memory of John Earl*. It should only be attempted when the sound is to be added to the film as a magnetic stripe or as composite optical print. The tape-recorded track played beside the projector will drift just enough to make the voices go out of sync. Audiences become uncomfortable when lip sync is more than three or four frames out of coordination with the picture.

How do you decide which sounds will go best with your film? I have noticed that most students become absolutely confident about what kind of track they want after a minimum of preliminary testing. Perhaps decisions about sound are made unconsciously during prior work on the film. The final selection is as personal a matter as choice of subject, manner of photography, and style of editing.

THERE WILL PROBABLY BE MANY MONTHS BETWEEN YOUR DECISION to make a film and your viewing of the finished print. During that period you will have formulated your ideas, learned how to use a camera, found appropriate locations and actors, shot the picture and titles, edited the film, and recorded and synchronized the sound track. The next step is an exciting one: showing your movie to an audience.

Some of my students have gone to great lengths to arrange a showing of their films. Randy and Andy convinced a local art gallery to give them use of a room for their screening. They talked to a reporter from their local newspaper and got advance publicity. They silk-screened banners and stickers, which they distributed all over town. They mailed invitations to friends. There was, as a result of all this, an excellent turnout. As so often happens, no matter how far ahead plans are made, the young filmmakers were still synchronizing the sound track and making last-minute picture cuts on the day of the screening.

Whether or not you choose to be so elaborate, there are several things to keep in mind. Be sure the room can be totally darkened and have it in subdued light until the picture begins so the audience's eyes will adjust effectively to screen illumination. Stagger rows of chairs so each person looks between the heads of the two people in front of him. Try to have the projector as far away from the audience as possible so its whirring is not audible; if the sound source can be separated from the projector, have the projector in another room, preferably shooting through a glass door. Ideally the sound should emanate from under the screen. Place the projector at least six feet above the floor so shadows from the audience's heads don't appear on screen. Avoid those dinky little home-movie screens measuring only three feet by four feet. The larger the image, the more impact your film will have, so screen size should be as big as you can make it. You can effectively use a white wall or a bed sheet hung on a wall; although these surfaces do not have the illuminating qualities of a standard beaded or lenticular movie screen, they make up in size for what they lack in brilliance.

When you are setting up the projector and screen, run the projector with the lamp on and without film to frame the picture accurately on screen. If you notice hairy or fuzzy shadows around the the edge of the rectangle of light on screen, it means the projector gate is clogged with dust and should be cleaned with a soft brush or dry cotton swab. While you are at it, remove the projector lens and clean it as you clean a camera lens. Always have on hand a spare projector lamp and, if your projector and film have optical sound, a spare exciter lamp.

Another accessory for the projectionist is a roll of quarter-inch masking tape in case the film breaks (as it may do where there has been a weak splice or if the film is not threaded properly on the projector). Never use celluloid tape because it is very hard to peel off, and after the screening you will want to repair the film on the splicer. Before the audience arrives, have the film in the projector with the first frame set at the projector gate in sharp focus. If your screening is away from home, refer to a checklist of things to take with you: extension cords, take-up reel, three-prong plug adaptor if you use a 16mm projector, cotton swab to clean projector gate, lens cleaner and cloth, quarter-inch masking tape, spare lamps for projector, screen or white sheet, and the film itself (inexperienced filmmakers have remembered everything but the film). Effectively organizing a screening reduces your anxiety and permits you to sit back and enjoy the occasion with the audience.

I have been trying to convey a sense of the exhilaration and fun that filmmaking can provide. If you find your interest challenged, you should now be able to make your own movie. Afterward, you will probably have technical questions beyond the scope of this book. Many professional filmmakers swear by the *American Cinematographer Manual*. It is a 625-page compilation of data essential to motion-picture production. The price is $12.50 postpaid, but periodically it goes up. If you can't get the book from your local bookstore, you can order it from:

A.S.C. Holding Corp.
1782 North Orange Drive
Hollywood, California 90028

It is well worth the cost if you wish to understand cinematography thoroughly.

If you plan to buy new Super-8 movie equipment, check out *Consumer Reports* for its recent listings. It is published in twelve monthly issues (available at newsstands and libraries) and these are in turn compiled in a year's-end paperback, *Buying Guide Issue* (available at bookstores and newsstands). The ratings are keyed to both quality and economy and are made after testing by Consumers Union, a non-profit organization.

Developed motion-picture film can be mailed at a special postal rate. State on the package, "Special Fourth Class Rate—Film." At this writing the cost is twelve cents for the first pound and six cents for each additional pound. First- and second-class mail take priority over fourth-class unless you send the package Special Handling; this costs twenty-five cents for up to two pounds, thirty-five cents for two to ten pounds, and fifty cents for over ten pounds. Postal insurance is twenty cents for up to $15, thirty cents for $15.01 to $50, and

165

forty cents for $50.01 to $100. Insure your film only for what you can prove, with receipts, that you spent in making it. Since postal rates do change, ask at the post office when you mail your film what the current rates are.

If you have any plans to make a profit on your completed film, there are some legal steps you should take. As long as you show the movie for fun, you may feel free of worry about legalities, but when profit from rental or sale is involved, you must protect yourself and respect the rights of others.

A release form (see sample, page 167), is required from every person who appears in the film. In documentaries and journalistic movies where dozens of passersby may be seen, release forms are customarily obtained on location only from central characters. To make the release legally binding, give each actor one dollar when he signs. In the sample release, you will read, "For good consideration, receipt of which is hereby acknowledged"; this refers to that dollar, and if you can't afford to pay it, cross out those words. If you want to devise a profit-sharing arrangement with participants in your film, it will be necessary for your parents to consult a lawyer because minors are not allowed to set up a business.

Your sound track may come under copyright laws. If you wish to include recorded music or voices that are copyrighted, write to the record company explaining how your film is to be used commercially and asking written permission to use their material. They may say no. If you can't persuade them, choose other music. Using original music gets around the problems of permission, but be sure to get musicians to sign the release form.

Why all these formalities? Laws have been designed for protection of the rights of individuals. Using a person's image commercially without his permission constitutes an invasion of his privacy. Composers, musicians, actors, and singers are professionals whose livelihoods de-

Name of filmmaker
Street address
City and state

                                        Date
                                        Name of film

Gentlemen:

For good consideration, receipt of which is hereby acknowledged, I hereby
grant to you, your successors, assigns, and licensees permission to use
any and all material that I write, direct, play, and/or photograph;
to photograph me, record my voice, reproduce and/or simulate my voice and
picture, and use my name, picture, and voice in and in connection with
the motion picture tentatively entitled the above name and in connection
with the distribution, exhibition, televising, exploitation, and
advertising thereof in any manner whatsoever in any part of the world.
I understand and agree that all services rendered by me in connection
with the above picture shall be fully and completely owned by you,
together with all of the results and proceeds of said services and that
I shall at no time own any rights to the above motion picture or portions
thereof and at no time shall I assert or make a claim against the above
motion picture for any reason whatsoever. I hereby release you from any
and all claims including, but not limited to, claims for libel and
invasion of privacy arising from my appearance in or services involving
the above motion picture whether arising from the actual exhibition or
other exploitation of the above motion picture or for any other reason
regardless of its nature. I acknowledge that the above grant is
irrevocable so that you may proceed in reliance thereon.

_____
Signature   Address   Date   Parent's or guardian's
                                                signature if signee is
                                                under twenty-one

pend on their skills and talents. By law they are entitled to profit from their works; they may choose to grant permission for it to be used to someone else's profit (yours).

Once you have acquired the various releases, you, too, own rights and they can be protected. Simply insert on the title of your film, "© Copyright," then your name and the year your film was finished. Have you wondered why on professional movies the year is in Roman numerals? It is so that audiences won't be able to read it and won't think a film made in an earlier year is old; they like the film they are watching to be fresh and new, unless it has become a classic. Any original work of art is generally protected by common law. You can protect yourself further in two ways. Before you start filming, send yourself by registered mail a copy of the treatment of the film you are going to make; do not open it (the sealed envelope with its registry mark is proof of ownership of the film described therein). Save your dated lab bill on which is noted the name of your film. I don't feel you need to go through the elaborate procedures necessary to register with the Copyright Office in Washington, D. C., unless you wish to bring suit against infringement of your copyright. In that case write for their form to:

Registrar of Copyright
Copyright Office
Library of Congress
Washington, D. C. 20540

This is a sample agreement between the owner of a film and a distribution corporation. It is legally binding on both parties. Elaborate contractual agreements are often drawn up, but this letter form is sufficient for a modest picture:

169

Date

Name of film owner
Street address
City and state

Dear _____ (Film owner):

This will confirm our conversation with regard to the distribution of
your film entitled _____; the following is our proposal:
1. We will distribute the film, to the 16mm nontheatrical
    market, for both rental and sale.
2. We propose to rent the 30-minute film for $25. The
    sale price will be $300.
3. We will prepare ___ pieces of publicity material
    with your assistance and approval and we will do
    mailing and publicity, in order to promote more
    extensive use of the film.
4. We propose to distribute the film under our name,
    giving you credit as producer.
5. We will share all income with you on a 50/50 basis,
    after the initial deduction to the amount of $___
    for print costs, preparations, and mailing of
    publicity material. We will render quarterly
    reports.
6. This agreement is to pertain to the World, for
    which we will be the exclusive distributor.
7. This agreement is valid for a period of five (5)
    years, commencing at once.
8. We will use our best efforts to sell this film
    to television stations and as a theatrical featurette.
    If we are able to consummate such a sale, we will
    discuss terms with you, which will be subject to
    your approval.
9. Our books may be audited by you upon request.
10. You warrant that you have all rights to this film
    (pix, music, etc.) in perpetuity.
If the above terms are agreeable to you, please sign one copy of this
agreement and return to us.

APPROVED _____
              Film owner

                                        Sincerely,

                              _____
                              Film distributor's name

Until very recently Americans, both young and adult, were not taking films made by teen-agers very seriously. Today there is a growing enthusiasm about these movies. Commercial distributors have not yet found a way to handle the legal details involved in doing business with minors. The Young Filmaker's Foundation, of which I am a co-director with Lynne Hofer and Jaime Barrios, is vitally interested in seeing films by young people distributed and producing a profit for their creators or for the workshops which sponsor them. In fact, one of the main objectives of the foundation is to provide information for schools, churches, libraries, community centers, and similar organizations about the activities of teen-age filmmakers. If you feel pleased by your film and are prepared to go through the copyright clearances and gain release forms, you might write to us for instructions about how to get your film distributed; we will send you updated suggestions. The address is:

Young Filmaker's Foundation
310 West 53rd Street
New York, N. Y. 10019

Don't be unduly concerned about copyrights and releases if your only goal is film festivals. There are several organizations to whom you can write for information about festivals. Here are three:

The American Film Institute
Education Division
1815 H Street, N.W.
Washington, D. C. 20006

CINE
16th Street, N.W.
Washington, D. C. 20036

171

International Centre of Films
    for Children and Young People
Secrétariat Général
241, rue Royale
Bruxelles 3, Belgium

The American Film Institute is a private nonprofit agency interested in all aspects of American filmmaking. CINE (Council on International Nontheatrical Events) is a government agency which screens films made in the United States and chooses entries for foreign film festivals; there is an amateur film section. The International Centre of Films arranges festivals all over the world for young people's movies.

Some months or years after your movie is completed you will discover that it has a life of its own. During production you feel in control of a film, but later on it seems separate from you. Contributing to this strange sensation may be an awareness that people you have never met have seen it. In any event, with time, the memory of all that went into its making becomes blurred, and the film rolls effortlessly and swiftly through the projector. Who knows exactly what your reaction will then be to this record of an adventure you once had?

Glossary

ANIMATION An illusion of motion given to drawings and inanimate objects by photographing them one or two frames at a time. The drawings appear to move when the film is projected onto a screen.

APERTURE Camera: Opening through which the lens projects the image onto the film as it runs through the camera's film gate. Lens: Opening through which light passes to film.

ASA RATING American Standards Association description of a film stock's tolerance to light.

B&W Black-and-white film stock or print.

BASE Clear acetate foundation of every film stock. Identified as shiny side of film.

CARTRIDGE Container of Super 8 film, which is inserted in Super 8 cameras. Similar device holds Super 8 prints for some projectors.

CINÉMA VÉRITÉ A style of moviemaking popularized by the French in which actors and nonactors are photographed spontaneously. Neither script nor studio is used.

CLOSE-UP A shot taken while camera and subject are near one another, so that subject's head and shoulders, for instance, fill frame in viewfinder.

COLOR BALANCE Proper amount and kind of light to expose color film accurately.

COPYRIGHT Legal registration of one's ownership of a creative work, *e.g.,* a song or a film.

CREDITS A listing of who has worked in and on the movie; it usually appears at the beginning or end.

CRITICAL FOCUS The exact distance from camera to subject as indicated on focusing ring of lens.

CUT Noun: Each piece of film that has been trimmed to the desired length. With a fast cut just a few frames remain in the shot when it has been spliced. Verb: To switch from one scene or angle to another.

DAILIES Prints from original footage as they are screened before they are cut. In a large production the director reviews each day's shooting the following day. Also called rushes because the print is rushed to the screening room as soon as it is ready.

174

DEPTH OF FIELD Those distances and objects from near to far that are in acceptably sharp focus.

DEVELOP The laboratory process that fixes the exposed film. Developing is also called processing. It is recommended that a professional film lab be used.

DIAPHRAGM An adjustable ring of metal surrounding the aperture. It changes size to regulate amount of light passing through lens.

DIRECT PHOTOGRAPHY Camera records live action.

DISSOLVE One image fades out and simultaneously the next one fades in. Sometimes called a lap dissolve.

DOCUMENTARY A film that attempts to record an event or situation factually and objectively.

DOUBLE EXPOSURE Film is run through camera twice to create two overlapping images. While this can be accidental, a purposeful overlap can be effectively created by filming the darker scene first.

DUB To add voices or sounds to a film that was shot with a silent camera. Or to add a different track from the original, as when dubbing into English a foreign-language movie shot in synchronous sound.

EDIT To assemble the various shots and sounds of a movie into a single continuous reel in the proper order and length.

EFFECTS Optical: Those scenes which are fabricated in printing the 16mm or 35 mm film after it has been developed. Dissolves, fade-outs and superimpositions are the most commonly applied. Sound: Reproduction of sounds other than voices or music, *e.g.,* sirens, animal cries, storms. Special: Images that are achieved by the use of miniature models, color filters in printing or other mechanical methods of photography.

ELECTRIC EYE Automatic, battery-powered light meter built into some cameras to set proper lens opening.

EMULSION Light-sensitive chemicals adhering to the film's acetate base. Identified as the dull side. These particles receive the image that is later fixed in developing.

ESTABLISHING SHOT The scene, often but not necessarily the first to be shown, that reveals the movie's location.

EXCITER LAMP The lamp in the projector producing a beam of light that passes through the optical sound track, sending impulses to the amplifier and so creating the sound for a movie as it is projected.

175

EXPOSE   To allow light to strike raw film stock, leaving its mark on the emulsion.

EXTREME CLOSE-UP   A very close shot of a detail, *e.g.,* a picture of a blinking eye or turning doorknob.

EXTREME LONG SHOT   A shot framed to extend as far as the camera can see. The lens focusing ring is set on infinity.

FADE-IN   An image begins in blackness and gradually becomes illuminated. The lens diaphragm is closed down as far as it will go and then slowly opens to proper exposure setting.

FADE-OUT   An image on the film gradually disappears into blackness. Achieved by reversing process described above. Both fade-in and fade-out can be mechanically produced in film printing machine.

FAST FILM   Film with a high ASA rating that is extremely sensitive to light. Best for filming where there is little light available. Also called high-speed film. Slow film needs bright light to expose properly. (Neither fast nor slow film refers to motion.)

FAST MOTION   Camera records fewer frames per second than is usual; projected, images move faster on screen than in reality.

FILM GATE   Camera: Track through which film passes behind aperture; it holds each frame in place for exposure. Projector: Track that holds film in front of projection lamp beam while film is projected.

FILM GAUGE   Width of film stock: Regular 8mm, Super 8mm, 16mm, 35mm, 70mm.

FILTER   Correction: Colored glass or gelatin that is inserted in lens or camera to alter quality of light striking film. For example, if indoor film is being used outdoors, a filter must be inserted to correct the daylight so that it resembles tungsten light. Neutral density: A filter which reduces the light intensity so that high speed film can be used in bright light.

FINE CUT   The complete assemblage of the movie. All shots are cut to proper length and spliced into correct order.

FIXED-FOCUS LENS   A lens that does not have a focusing adjustment but records almost all distances with reasonable clarity.

FOCAL LENGTH   The distance, measured in millimeters, from the center of the lens to the surface of the film in the camera. Wide-angle lenses have a short length, telephotos have a long one.

176

FOCUS   To set a camera or projector lens so that the image being made on the film or on the screen is sharply defined.

FOLLOW FOCUS   The subject is kept in focus as it moves by adjusting the lens focusing ring while filming.

FOOTAGE   A film print before it is cut.

FRAME   Noun: A single picture on a length of film. Pictures are separated by a narrow frame line at the sprocket hole. Verb: To compose the picture area in the viewfinder of the camera.

FPS   Frames per second. The number of pictures produced each second as the film passes through the camera gate during filming.

FREEZE FRAME   A single frame of the action is printed repeatedly in the film printing machine, and that picture appears to be absolutely still on the screen as the film runs through the projector.

F/STOP   The size of the lens aperture opening: 1.4, 2., 2.8, 4. (wide openings); 5.6, 8., 11. (medium openings); 16., 22. (small openings).

GRAIN   The chemical particles of the film's emulsion that are seen as pulsating dot patterns when the picture is greatly enlarged on screen. Fast films have a coarse grain; slow films have a fine grain.

HEAD (OF FILM)   Beginning of a shot. The editor locates a person's head or the sky to find the head of a shot.

INFINITY   Extreme distances from camera, beyond focusing control of lens. All that the camera is capable of recording far away will be in focus when lens focusing ring is set to infinity, but nearby objects will be out of focus.

INSERT   A detail shot that will be spliced into a scene to give more information. For example, in a poker-game sequence, a player's hand of cards may be shown to let the audience in on who is winning.

INTERCUT   To shift back and forth between two or more scenes, usually to show that they are taking place simultaneously. Also called parallel construction.

JUMP CUT   Action is spliced together that is not carefully matched; this has a jarring effect on the audience. Some scenes may be improved by this method, but ordinarily film editors wish to have the action carry through a cut smoothly.

LEADER   A blank strip of film spliced to the beginning and end of every reel of film. Head leader permits threading of the projector without losing first frames of picture. Tail leader is attached to prevent final picture frames from being torn as the tail of film leaves the projector.

LIGHT METER   An instrument that measures light intensity and relates this measurement to the film's sensitivity to insure proper exposure. Incident meters record the light as it falls on the subject. Reflected meters record the light as it reflects off the subject.

LIP SYNC   Talking pictures where the picture of lip movements synchronizes with voices on the sound track.

LOADING SPOOL   Some Regular 8 and most 16mm film come wound on a spool that can be loaded into the camera in subdued light. The film is threaded manually around the camera's sprocket wheels, through the film gate, and onto the take-up spool.

MAGAZINE   A sealed container of film, which is opened only in the laboratory after exposure. Some Regular 8 cameras use a 25′ magazine load and some old 16mm cameras use a 50′ magazine load; these are inserted into the camera. A 100′ 16 mm spool can be developed for the same price as a 50′ 16mm magazine load. Electric motor driven 16mm cameras may use 400′ or 1,200′ magazines, which are mounted on top of the camera body for long continuous shooting and which are not sealed containers.

MAGNETIC SOUND   A recording on quarter-inch tape may be transferred to a magnetic stripe on 8mm or 16mm film and played on a projector with a magnetic sound head. Or it may be transferred to a 16mm magnetic sprocketed tape to be aligned with the picture before an optical track is made, in which case the sound is again transferred and becomes a visible wiggly line on the edge of the film print.

MASTER SHOT   A shot that encompasses all the significant action, filmed continuously and usually taken at some distance with a stationary camera. Later the scene is often shot from additional angles and with visual attention to small details.

MATCH CUT   A splice that smoothly joins two pieces of action that were shot from different angles. There is continuity of action, and the audience is seldom aware that there has been a change of camera position.

MEDIUM SHOT   A shot from medium distance. An actor is seen from the top of his head to his waist only.

MIX   Two or more individual sound tracks, such as music and narration,

178

may be played through a mixer to produce a composite sound track that combines the individual sounds of each track.

MOVIEOLA   A highly professional motor-driven editing machine, which locks pictures and 16mm magnetic tapes together for cutting and sync-sound pictures.

NEGATIVE FILM   A 16mm B&W film stock in which white appears black. A work print must be made for the white of the subject to appear white.

NORMAL LENS   A lens whose scope is similar to that of human vision.

OPTICAL TRACK   Sound is reduced to a fine wiggly line printed on the edge of a 16mm film print on the side opposite the sprocket holes. In the projector, when a beam of light passes through the optical track, impulses are sent to the projector's amplifier and the sound becomes audible.

OUT-OF-FOCUS   Picture is blurred and indistinct because lens was not set for the subject's distance from it.

OUTTAKES   Scenes shot that the editor does not plan to include in the movie. They should be carefully stored in case he changes his mind.

OVEREXPOSE   To allow too much light to strike the film's emulsion during filming. This causes the image to appear pale and washed out.

PAINTED FILM   Color is applied directly to film that has first had all the emulsion removed with a Clorox bath. Acetate inks and indelible markers are often used because they are compatible with the film's base. No camera is involved.

PAN   To move the camera horizontally or vertically, following a moving subject or taking in a larger expanse than could be seen if the camera remained stationary. Beginners tend to overdo panning and should consider cutting together parts of a scene, rather than constantly swinging the camera around.

PARALLAX CORRECTION   Viewfinders that do not see directly through the camera lens have correcting devices to approximate the frame as recorded on the film. The closer the subject to the lens, the more correction is required.

PHOTOFLOOD LAMP   Tungsten light used for nighttime or indoor illumination.

PISTOL GRIP   An alternative to a tripod for steadying the camera while filming. Particularly useful on lightweight cameras, it allows the cameraman to hold the camera firmly in his hands by a grip handle attached to the camera base.

PIXILATION   Single-frame shooting of people, or of people interacting with objects, which gives the moving image an unreal, eerie motion.

PRINT   A duplicate made (or struck) from the original film that went through the camera and has been developed. A work print is a copy from the uncut original and is used for editing. Later the original is cut to match frame-by-frame the fine cut made from the work print. Using a work print spares the original from damage during editing. When the sound track is printed on the edge of the picture, the result is called a composite print. A release print is a copy of the original film edited for public showing.

READING   The measurement of light intensity as it registers on the light meter.

REFLECTED PHOTOFLOOD   A tungsten lamp with a reflective base that concentrates the light it throws.

RELEASE   A legal consent form in which those who appear in a film give their permission for their images or voices to be used.

REVERSAL FILM   All 8mm and 16mm color and much B&W film are of the reversal type. White remains white on original reversal, for the negative image was reversed in developing; it can be projected (a print does not have to be made first).

REVERSE ANGLE   A scene is shown in continuous action first from one side and then from the opposite side (a 180 degree angle change of camera position) through a cut.

REWIND   An editing tool with a manually turned spindle on which a reel of film is placed. A set of two is required to move the film through a viewer or splicer; the lefthand rewind holds the feed-off reel while the righthand one holds the take-up reel. When rewinding 16mm film after showing it on a projector, it is best to use these manual rewinds rather than to rewind the film in the projector because rewinding puts strain on the projector's mechanisms.

ROUGH CUT   A first assemblage of the film; some shots are still too long and some are out of place.

SCENARIO   A detailed description of the movie to be made, which includes camera angles, locations, and dialogue.

180

SCRATCH FILM   Film that has been developed so that its emulsion is black. Designs are scratched through the emulsion to the base with a stylus. No camera is involved.

SCREEN   Beaded: The surface of the screen is composed of tiny glass beads, which provide the projected images with increased brilliance. Lenticular: A metallic, ridged surface on a screen, which also intensifies the illumination of the projected image.

SCREEN TIME   An action seems to take more time on screen than it does in reality.

SCREENING   The presentation of a film to an audience.

SHOOTING SCRIPT   A breakdown of the script into a specific filming schedule that does not follow the order of the plot but is based on practical shooting requirements. Only when the film is later edited will its sequences be in the proper order.

SHOULDER BRACE   The camera is attached to a brace that rests on the cameraman's shoulder. It allows him more mobility than if the camera were on a tripod. Most helpful when using a heavy camera.

SHUTTER   Positioned between the camera aperture and film gate, it is a device for closing out light while film moves from one frame to the next. A variable shutter is one whose opening may be adjusted to let in more or less light. Shutters are also found in film viewers and projectors and provide an instant of darkness between frames.

SHUTTER RELEASE   The button on the camera which, when pushed, activates the camera motor and so the shutter.

SLOW MOTION   Camera records more frames per second than is usual; projected, the images move more slowly on screen than in reality.

SOUND HEAD   The drum around which the sound, either magnetic or optical, passes as it sends its signal to the amplifier.

SOUND TRACK   All sounds used with a movie. Played from a nearby tape recorder or from the sound head of the projector.

SPLICE   To join two pieces of film by overlapping and cementing the edge of the tail of the first shot to the head of the second. This is called a wet splice and is recommended over the film butt splice which is made by butting the tail to the head and taping them with sprocketed mylar tape. Magnetic tape may also be spliced; the splice is diagonal, and it is butted and taped.

181

SPLICER   The machine that trims and locks two pieces of film or sound tape together so they can be joined with cement or tape.

SPRING-WIND CAMERA   A camera with a motor driven by a coiled spring rather than by electric power. It must be rewound manually after each shot.

SPROCKET HOLES   The small holes or perforations along the edge of the film that allow it to be pulled through the projector and camera gate over the sprocket wheels.

STOCK   Film before it has been exposed or recording tape before it has been recorded. Both are also called raw stock.

STORYBOARD   A series of sketches of the movie being planned, often resembling a comic strip.

SUBJECTIVE CAMERA   The camera seems to be looking out on the action through the eyes of a character in the movie.

SUN GUN   An especially bright tungsten lamp designed to illuminate poorly lit interiors. Also used out of doors on facial close-ups to soften harsh shadows on bright days.

SWISH PAN   A fast horizontal movement of the camera during filming which gives a streaked or blurred picture. Used to suggest a speedy transition from one place to another.

SYNCHRONIZER   A metal, manually operated machine that has two or more sprocket wheels on which are locked 16mm film and 16mm magnetic sprocketed tape, in order to align picture and sound. It is placed between a pair of rewinds.

SYNCHRONOUS SOUND   Sound that matches the picture precisely. It requires electric sync motor-driven camera and tape recorder. Too expensive and complicated for beginners.

TAIL (OF FILM)   The end of a film strip. Recognized by looking at the bottom edge of a frame and locating grass or actors' feet.

TELEPHOTO LENS   A lens that brings distant objects extremely close and shortens the depth of a scene.

TRACKING SHOT   Camera moves while filming. Cameraman may be walking, pushed in a wheelchair, pulled in a wagon, or riding in a car as he shoots.

TRANSITION SHOT   A length of picture spliced in to carry the movie smoothly from one scene to the next.

182

TREATMENT   A general outline of a movie idea which suggests the characters, situations, and locations.

TRIMS   Those lengths of film that are removed from the rough cut as the movie approaches its finished form.

TRIPOD   A portable three-legged stand on which the camera can be mounted for extremely steady pictures. It can be adjusted for various heights and is equipped with a pan handle so that the mounted camera can be pivoted either horizontally or vertically.

TURRET   Rotating plate on the front of a camera holding two or more lenses so that any one lens may be placed over the camera aperture without removing the others from the camera.

UNDEREXPOSE   To allow too little light to strike the film's emulsion during filming. This causes the image to appear dark and obscure.

VIEWER   The machine that allows the editor to view the film at his own tempo while he is assembling the movie and making editorial decisions.

VIEWFINDER   The rectangle through which the cameraman looks to frame his subject. A parallax viewfinder only approximates the lens' view of the subject. A reflex viewfinder uses the lens itself and so gives greater accuracy in framing; it also allows the cameraman to see if the subject is out of focus.

WIDE-ANGLE LENS   A lens that widens the view of the scene and increases the depth unrealistically.

ZOOM LENS   A lens that varies its focal length over a continuous range, making it possible to slide between establishing shot and close-up in a single shot; the lens moves from wide angle (12mm) through normal (25mm) to telephoto (120mm).

Acknowledgments

Following is a complete list of the films by young people discussed in the book.

A Day in the Life by Josué Hernandez
    starring Miguel Sanchez with Naomi Hernandez

A Park Called Forsyth by Jesus Cruz
    with Pedro Castro, Alfonso Sanchez, Ray Esquilin, and Rosalene Phillips

An Unpleasant Evening by Jesus Cruz
    with Rosalene Phillips, Pedro Castro, and Ivan Quiles

The Breakfast by Karen Wolf
    with Judith Kurtz and Bernard Neri

Bubby by Murray Kramer
    starring "Bubby" Fishman with Susan Schmulowitz

Cecile Comes to Southampton by Andy Gurian
    with the Erland family, Michele Karmazin, Steve Kahn, Peter Poulson, and . . . Cecile

Circus by Ronald Cogle

Diana by Fran Hassan
    starring Elin Scheiber with Maxine Hassan

The Ed Skullivan Show by Alvin Thomas

Flash by José Colon
    starring Alejandro and David Lopez

The Flop by Luis Valé
    with Ray Ossorio and Max Perez

Life Is Just a Bowl of Cherries by Susan Whyne

Look at Me by Cathy Simpson

Looking Back by Benjamin Katz

Memory of John Earl by John Earl McFadden

That Rotten Teabag by Andy Gurian
    with Randy Pelton, Arlene Alexander, and Dorothy Cooper

The End by Alfonso Sanchez, Jr.
  starring Benny Hernandez with Robert Bonilla and Frankie Merced

The Revenge—Teenagers Western Style, Miguel Sanchez, student director;
  produced by Jaime Barrios and Rodger Larson
  with Alfonso Sanchez, Jesus Cruz, Pedro Castro, Robert Bonilla, Rosalene Phillips, Ishmal Otero, and Julie Hammid

The Tell-Tale Heart by William Ostrow
  with Bill Stewart, Harvey Schafer, and Sandor Tepper

Those Powerful Pills by Miguel Sanchez
  starring José Colon

untitled animation experiments by Peter Wallach

untitled scratch film by Randy Pelton

Yesterday by Paul Tepper
  with Joe Dee and Susan Bauer

Many of these films are currently in distribution. For information write to
Young Filmaker's Foundation, 310 West 53rd Street, New York, New
York 10019.

Young filmmakers (all members of FILM CLUB) who appear in Marcelo
Montealegre's photographs throughout the book are as follows: title page:
Steven Dobbs, Jayson R. Wcchtcr, Stanleigh Williams; p. 65: José Colon;
p. 84: Raphael Colon; p. 97: Luis Valé; p. 99: Raphael Colon; p. 111:
Jayson R. Wechter; p. 114: Harvey Cowen, Jayson R. Wechter; p. 117:
Shelton Ray, Jayson R. Wechter; p. 118: Harvey Cowen, Shelton Ray;
p. 120: Jayson R. Wechter, Stanleigh Williams, Steven Dobbs, Harvey
Cowen; p. 122: Jayson R. Wechter; p. 124: Harvey Cowen, Steven Dobbs,
Drexel Harris; p. 126: Harvey Cowen, Shelton Ray; p. 127: Steven Dobbs,
Shelton Ray, Stanleigh Williams, Harvey Cowen, Jayson R. Wechter;
p. 134: Alfonso Pagán-Cruz; p. 136: Luis Valé; p. 141: Bryan Dennard;
p. 159: Marizel Rios, José Colon; p. 168: Linell Banks, Jr.; p. 173: Alfonso
Pagán-Cruz, Raphael Colon.

Index

187

188

trick photography, 34-35. *See also* special effects

trims, 148, 183

triple exposure, 57

tripod, 32, 43, 82-83, 87, illus. 111, 183

tungsten light, 89, 98, table 100-101

turret, 94, 183

2001: A Space Odyssey, 57

underexpose, 89, 183

University Settlement, 13

Unpleasant Evening, An, 25-28, illus. 26, 76

Upward Bound, 21, 23

viewer, film, 144-146, illus. 147, 183

viewfinder, 80, 183

Warhol, Andy, 14, 66, 138

Wesleyan University, 21

wide-angle lens, 57, 94, 183

work print, 90, 148, 158

Yesterday, 61-63, illus. 62

Young Filmaker's Foundation, 13, 171

zoom lens, 57, 94, 105, 183

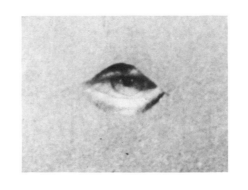